PITMAN SHORTERHAND

Revised Edition

GEORGE A. REID, B. Comm., B.Ed., M.A., F.C.C.T.
Professor, Business Education Department
The Faculty of Education, University of Toronto

EVELINA J. THOMPSON, B.A., B.Ed.
Chairman, Secretarial Science Department
Ryerson Polytechnical Institute, Toronto

Edited by MARION ANGUS,
Business Education Consultant
Pitman Publishing

Copp Clark Pitman
A division of Copp Clark Limited
Toronto

ISBN 0-7730-4126-5

AUSTRALIA—Pitman Publishing Pty. Ltd., Melbourne
U.K.—Pitman Publishing Ltd., London
NEW ZEALAND—Pitman Publishing, New Zealand Ltd.
U.S.A.—Fearon-Pitman Publishers Inc., Belmont, California
EAST AFRICA—Sir Isaac Pitman Ltd., Nairobi, Kenya
SOUTH AFRICA—Pitman Publishing Co. SA (Pty.) Ltd., Johannesburg

Cover photo by Paul Buer
Printed and bound in Canada

Copp Clark Pitman
517 Wellington Street West
Toronto, Ontario
M5V 1G1

Acknowledgements

A work of the nature of SHORTERHAND, introducing a modification of the basic principles of a famous system of shorthand, is dependent upon the contributions and assistance of many individuals and organizations. The authors wish to express their sincere appreciation to all those who contributed to the development of this project. Our special thanks are extended to the many teachers and their numerous students in the secondary schools and the Colleges of Applied Arts and Technology of Ontario who contributed their time, skill, and knowledge to enable us to compile a critical evaluation of the system and to prepare this text. We wish also to express our appreciation to the officials of the Curriculum Branches of the provincial Departments of Education for their encouragement and advice.

Our sincere appreciation is extended to the Pitman Company for its support, advice, and encouragement in the development of this modified version of its famous shorthand system. In particular, acknowledgement is given to the shorthand experts of the Company who gave of their time and advice.

Finally, the authors wish to acknowledge their debt to Sir Isaac Pitman, the inventor of classic Pitman shorthand, upon whose genius the success of the whole system is based.

G.A.R.
E.J.T.

Introduction

The Pitman system of shorthand is a system unequalled for its speed potential and accuracy of transcription.

Sir Isaac Pitman published his shorthand system in 1837. Through the years this original version has been revised and modified through many editions. This new text, SHORTERHAND, offers for the first time, an extensively *simplified* as well as modified version while retaining the fundamental principles of the classic Pitman system.

In this text there are 28 lessons, each one designed to promote effective learning in small segments. The theory of the system is presented through a series of Pitman Principles and each principle is fully illustrated by examples. These examples, plus many others, are then automatized in contextual exercise material giving the student a practical application of the theory through reading, writing, and dictation practice.

The introduction of transcription practice as early as Lesson 3 is a very important innovation so far as Pitman shorthand texts are concerned. The student now has the opportunity of immediately discovering the purpose and value of learning shorthand.

The modification as presented in this text is intended to:

(1) Reduce the time required to teach the basic theory by approximately 50 percent.

(2) Develop a high level of shorthand reading ability.

(3) Develop rapid shorthand writing from the early stages of learning.

(4) Make the student conscious of the vital importance of a knowledge of English as related to transcription.

The prime aims of the text are to develop a high level of speed in writing shorthand and the ability to transcribe accurately. Through a carefully planned study approach shown in the Skill-Building Plans, it is expected that when students have completed a study of the 28 lessons they will be taking dictation on familiar material at 80 words a minute, transcribing this material quickly and accurately. After completing a study of this text, students will be able to further develop their skills through continued study of this system at a more advanced level.

Plan of Text

The 28 lessons of the text have been carefully designed to make learning easy and effective. Lessons are divided into Units, each one with a specific purpose:

Unit 1 introduces *Pitman Principles* with examples.

Unit 2 introduces *Pitman Pacers* which are special signs representing very frequently used words.

Unit 3 introduces reading and writing practice material.

Unit 4 introduces material for developing transcription skill.

While there is some slight variation in this overall plan, these units are essentially the basis of the text.

In the belief that learning should be made as easy as possible, there is a key for all material immediately available following the shorthand.

The Skill-Building Plans, which are repeated throughout the text, give specific suggestions for the development of skill in all aspects of shorthand writing and transcription.

Skill-Building Plan 1 gives suggestions for the learning of the principles of the system through the reading and writing of outlines.

Skill-Building Plan 2 gives suggestions for building reading, writing, and dictation skills through practice on letters and other contextual material.

Skill-Building Plan 3 gives suggestions for the development of the transcription skill.

These plans are designed to help both students and teachers.

The Skill-Building Plans appear in Lessons 1, 2, 3, 4, 5, 7, 10, 15, 20, and 24. The speed aim indicated with the plans gradually increases throughout the text. At the end of each Unit a short note directs the student to the appropriate study plan for that Unit.

This *Shorterhand* text represents a new approach in Pitman shorthand texts. The theory of the system is presented primarily through the inductive teaching method. However, no matter which method is used, success is always dependent on the skill and experience of the teacher. In addition, every teacher must be free to select the method, or combination of methods, which in his experience have resulted in effective learning. It is with these beliefs in mind that the text has been designed so that it provides for flexibility and freedom of choice on the part of the teacher.

In designing the text the following principles were considered of major importance:

1. The teaching and learning of shorthand must involve reading and writing from plate shorthand and writing from dictation at a rate that challenges the students but does not discourage them – a speed requiring that outlines be written, not drawn.

2. Shorthand is not a problem-solving subject.

3. Learning should be made as easy as possible. The use of a key is therefore considered an essential part of each lesson.

4. Transcription should be introduced early in the learning process.

In the majority of lessons, the theory of the system is presented in such a way that the student discovers the principles of the system through the examples given in the text. This method – usually termed the discovery or inductive approach – is only one of the many ways in which the theory of the system may be taught. It is quite possible that some teachers and some students will prefer a more traditional approach. The format has been designed to permit the experienced teacher to use any method which has produced effective learning. At the same time, it is felt that the format will be of practical help to the new teacher. It is designed to provide maximum flexibility to both teacher and student.

The Word Family Principle

The theory of the system is presented through the word family principle. This principle encourages ease of learning and emphasizes the fact that similar sounds are represented by similar symbols. By using the word family plan it is possible to learn one basic outline and to build a shorthand vocabulary very easily by simple additions to the basic outline. The word family presentation also provides students with the necessary repetitive practice in a way that prevents boredom. The modifications presented in *Shorterhand* make it possible to introduce a much larger grouping of word families than was possible in texts for the classic system. The use of the word family principle reduces the possibilities of shorthand becoming a problem-solving subject.

The Study Program

The use of Skill-Building Plans gives both students and teachers a program of studies designed to ease the learning and teaching load. These features may be used for classroom teaching, for homework assignments, or for review. Since they present a clear and logical approach to the learning of the system, the Plans will prove valuable to the new teacher, to the regular student working on homework assignments or review studies, and to the individual engaged in private study.

The Use of the Key

Another feature of the text is the use of a key – or transcript – in conjunction with the shorthand material. In each lesson, where the examples of the shorthand outlines illustrating a new principle are presented, the printed word appears under each outline. Derivations of the root word are also shown. The grouping of words in word families shows the close relationship of each word in the family and the variations in spellings, where applicable, of the members of each family. This feature is designed to assist in the development of accurate spelling, an essential part of the transcription skill.

Contextual material is presented in each unit of every lesson through sentences, paragraphs, and letters. The key to all this material is given in the same lesson, usually in the last Unit. Presenting a key in conjunction with the shorthand material allows students to make rapid checks when outlines cause difficulties. The key is, of course, of great value to students studying alone. The location of the key closely following the shorthand enables students to concentrate on the main purpose of home study – the reading and writing of the shorthand. In this way the frustration of prolonged analysis and frequent defeat is eliminated. The decision to include the key with the material in the text was based on the psychological principle that learning, particularly in the early stages of a skill, should be made as easy as possible and initial frustrations reduced to the minimum.

All material in the sentences, paragraphs and letters is counted at an intensity of 1.4 syllables and marked for timed dictation at 14 syllables every 10 seconds by using the superior figures 10, 20, 30, 40, etc. The vocabulary count is therefore controlled. This control serves to make the material more meaningful in the development of shorthand writing.

The Introduction of Transcription

The introduction of transcription in Lesson 3 makes the purpose of learning shorthand immediately apparent to students who may now put their newly-acquired skill to immediate use. The early introduction of transcription not only improves the transcription skill at the end of the course, but also helps students to retain interest by providing additional motivation.

The teaching of the transcription skills is always the last unit in a lesson. The location of this unit is a further example of the flexibility which the design of the text offers to the teacher. Since the development of transcription skills appears at the end of each lesson, it is possible to omit this unit at the theory-learning stage, and to teach it at a later date without interfering with any other part of the lesson. The choice must always rest with the teacher.

The Transcription Skill-Building Plan

The Transcription Skill-Building Plan consists of three steps. As students progress through the text, the first two introductory steps are dropped, and the transcription proceeds directly from the dictation.

Skill-Building Plans 1 and 2 require students to read, write, and then to take from dictation the exercise material presented in the lesson. The Transcription Skill-Building Plan continues practice on the same familiar material. In Step 1 of the Transcription Skill-Building Plan, the students type from the letterpress key, the exercise material with which they are already familiar. In Step 2, the material is to be typed from plate shorthand. In Step 3, the material is dictated at a speed within the students' controlled ability – the level is best left to the judgement of the teacher – and students then transcribe this from their personal shorthand notes.

At Lesson 10, Step 1 of this plan is dropped and students transcribe first from the plate shorthand and then from the material which has been dictated. At Lesson 20, transcription from the plate shorthand is also dropped and students transcribe directly from their own notes. In this way the skill of transcription is acquired through the use of thoroughly familiar material in three easy stages. As the skill of the learner develops, the supporting steps in the process are removed. Of course, this plan can be modified by the teacher to meet the needs of a particular class.

When students have completed this beginning text they will:

(1) have completed the basic theory easily and quickly

(2) be able to write familiar material from dictation at 80 words per minute

(3) be able to transcribe this material quickly and accurately

(4) have the ability to initiate new outlines

(5) be in a position to further develop their shorthand skills through studies at an advanced level.

Table of Contents

1

Writing the sounds of P, B, T, D; vowels Ā, Ō; and Circle S

1 -17

1 - 4

UNIT 1

When we write shorthand we write signs only for the sounds we hear. We use a simple sign to represent each sound in our language. As we write, we are not concerned with the spelling of a word, but only with its sound.

Principle Discovery

We write the outline for the word *ate* by using only two signs ⸰⎸; a light stroke for the sound of T, and a dot for the sound of Ā.
We write the outline for the word *aid* by using only two signs ⸰⎸ , a dark stroke for the sound of D, and a dot for the sound of AI.

If the sounds heard in the word *aids* are represented by three signs ⸰⎸, can you discover the shorthand signs and principles used to write the sounds in the words listed below?

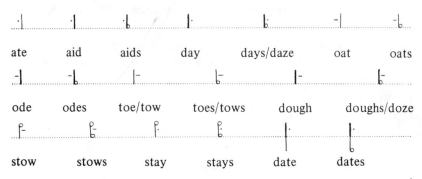

ate	aid	aids	day	days/daze	oat	oats

ode	odes	toe/tow	toes/tows	dough	doughs/doze

stow	stows	stay	stays	date	dates

1

Pitman Principles

1. T, a lightly sounded consonant, is a light straight stroke written downward ↓ as in *ate* ∵⌐ .

2. D, a strongly sounded consonant, is a dark straight stroke written downward ↓ as in *aid* ∴⌐ .

3. The sign for the vowel sound Ā is a dot. The sign for the vowel sound Ō is a dash.

4. The vowel signs are written before the stroke if they are sounded before as in *aid* ∴⌐ and *oat* ⌐ . They are written after the stroke if they are sounded after as in *day* ⌐ and *tow* ⌐ .

5. The sound S or Z is shown by a *small* circle written where it is sounded. If it is the first sound in a word write it first as in *stay* ℗ and *stow* ℗ : if it is the last sound write it last as in *tows* ᕐ .

READING TIP Always read from left to right →and from top to bottom ↓ . If a vowel comes first read it first as in *aid* ∵⌐ and *aids* ᕐ . If a vowel comes after read it after as in *day* ⌐ and *days* ᕐ . If it comes between strokes read it between as in *date* ⌐ and *dates* ᕐ .

SKILL-BUILDING PLAN I

Reading and Writing Practice

1. Read the shorthand outlines in this Unit, **preferably repeating the words out loud.**

2. Cover the printed words and read the shorthand outlines.

3. Write the shorthand outlines in your notebook until you can write them easily and quickly.

4. Write the shorthand outlines from dictation. Keep your text open as you write. Refer to your text for assistance whenever necessary.

5. Read the shorthand you have taken from dictation.

UNIT 2

Principle Discovery

> If the word *pay* is written ＼
>
> If the word *bay* is written ＼

can you discover the shorthand signs and principles used in writing the outlines for the words listed below?

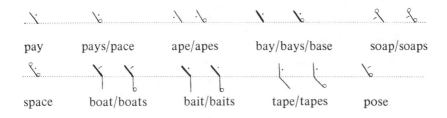

pay	pays/pace	ape/apes	bay/bays/base	soap/soaps
space	boat/boats	bait/baits	tape/tapes	pose

Pitman Principles

1. P, a lightly sounded consonant, is a light straight stroke written downward ＼ as in *pay* ＼ .
2. B, a strongly sounded consonant, is a dark straight stroke written downward ＼ as in *bay* ＼ .
3. Two or more strokes in a word are written without lifting the pen. Always write the strokes first:

> as in *boat* ＼ ; then insert the vowel sign ＼
>
> as in *tape* ∟ ; then insert the vowel sign ∟

READING TIP When you are reading a new word, *say* each sound exactly as you *hear* it. Train your ear to listen for the sounds which each sign represents. You will then be able to read the outline ＼ as B Ō T, or BŌAT — *not* BEE Ō TEE.

Master the outlines in Unit 2 by following Skill-Building Plan 1 on page 2.

2 Writing the sound of ING

UNIT 1

Principle Discovery

The sound ING is a very common word ending. Read the following outlines and discover the sign which represents ING:

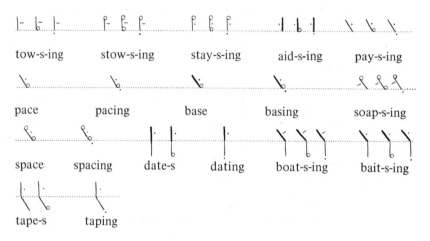

| tow-s-ing | stow-s-ing | stay-s-ing | aid-s-ing | pay-s-ing |

| pace | pacing | base | basing | soap-s-ing |

| space | spacing | date-s | dating | boat-s-ing | bait-s-ing |

| tape-s | taping |

Pitman Principles

1. A dot placed at the end of an outline represents the sound of ING.
2. Write the outline as follows:
   1. write the stroke ＼
   2. write the ING ＼
   3. write the vowel ＼

4

Reading and Writing Practice

1. Read the shorthand outlines in this Unit, **preferably repeating the words out loud.**
2. Cover the printed words and read the shorthand outlines.
3. Write the shorthand outlines in your notebook until you can write them easily and quickly.
4. Write the shorthand outlines from dictation. Keep your text open as you write. Refer to your text for assistance whenever necessary.
5. Read the shorthand you have taken from dictation.

UNIT 2

Pitman Pacers

Certain words are used so frequently in our language that we have special signs to represent them.

Pitman Pacers are short outlines representing these commonly used words. Because they set the pace for speed development we call them PITMAN PACERS.

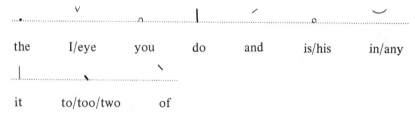

the	I/eye	you	do	and	is/his	in/any

it	to/too/two	of

Master the Pacers by following Skill-Building Plan 1 above.

UNIT 3

Phrases

Two or more outlines may be joined without lifting your pen to make outlines called *phrases*. The ability to write phrases easily and naturally is one of the secrets of high-speed writing. Phrasing should, however, be used only when outlines join naturally and can be read back without difficulty.

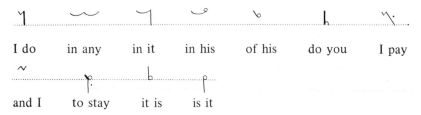

I do	in any	in it	in his	of his	do you	I pay

and I	to stay	it is	is it

Always write the first sign in a phrase in its correct position.
Note the use of a tick to express *the* in phrases. It is always written with a sharp angle.

in the	to the	is the	it is the	of the	tow the	and the

Master the Phrases by following Skill-Building Plan 1 on page 5.

PUNCTUATION TIPS Two light dashes under an outline indicate a proper name as in Abe ＼ and Babe ＼

The shorthand sign for a period is ⋯×⋯
The shorthand sign for a question mark is ⋯ʔ⋯

UNIT 4

SKILL-BUILDING PLAN 2

Building Reading and Writing Skills

1. Read each sentence until you can read it fluently.
2. Read all the sentences as a unit.
3. Practise writing each sentence in shorthand until you can write it easily and rapidly.
4. Write all the sentences once as a unit.

Building Dictation Skills

1. Practise writing each sentence from dictation. Keep your text open for easy reference.
2. Read the shorthand you have written in your notebook.

YOUR AIM: TO WRITE 50 WORDS IN A MINUTE

Reading and Writing Practice

Key to Reading and Writing Practice

1. I pay to tow the boat to the bay.[7]
2. I pay you to tow the boat to the bay.[7]
3. You and I tow the boat to the base in the bay.[9]
4. The tape is in the space in the base of the boat.[9]
5. Do you pay to stay in the boat? I do pay to stay in[10] it. Do I pay you?
6. Stow the bait in the boat. Abe is stowing the bait in the[10] space in the boat in the bay.[15]
7. Do you pay Babe to stay in the boat in the bay? Is it[10] in the base in the bay?[15]
8. Babe is staying in the boat. You and I stay in the boat,[10] too.
9. Is Abe staying in his boat? Abe is staying in his boat[10] in the bay.
10. Babe is stowing the bait and the tape in the space in the[10] base of his boat.

3

Writing the sounds of K, G, M, N

UNIT 1

Principle Discovery

If the word *ache* is written ___

If the word *gay* is written ___

If the word *aim* is written ___

If the word *nose* is written ___

can you discover the shorthand signs and principles used in writing the outlines for the words listed below?

> **READING TIP** Remember, we read from left to right and from top to bottom. Therefore, if the vowel sound comes first, read it first as in *ache* ↓ ___ . If the vowel sound comes after, read it after as in *gay* ↓ ___ .

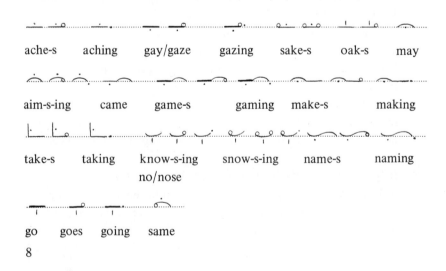

| ache-s | aching | gay/gaze | gazing | sake-s | oak-s | may |

| aim-s-ing | came | game-s | gaming | make-s | making |

| take-s | taking | know-s-ing | snow-s-ing | name-s | naming |
| | | no/nose | | | |

| go | goes | going | same |

8

Pitman Principles

1. K is a light, straight horizontal stroke as in *case* ......o.
2. G is a dark, straight horizontal stroke as in *gaze* ......o.
3. M is a light, curved horizontal stroke as in *aim* ⌒.
4. N is a light, curved horizontal stroke as in *know* ⌒.

SKILL-BUILDING PLAN I

Reading and Writing Practice

1. Read the shorthand outlines in this Unit, **preferably repeating the words out loud.**
2. Cover the printed words and read the shorthand outlines.
3. Write the shorthand outlines in your notebook until you can write them easily and quickly.
4. Write the shorthand outlines from dictation. Keep your text open as you write. Refer to your text for assistance whenever necessary.
5. Read the shorthand you have taken from dictation.

UNIT 2

Pitman Pacers

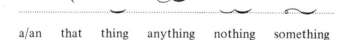

a/an   that   thing   anything   nothing   something

Phrases

that is   I know   I know the   I know that   I know that the   to go

Master the outlines in this Unit by following Skill-Building Plan 1 above.

UNIT 3

SKILL-BUILDING PLAN 2

Building Reading and Writing Skills

1. Read each sentence until you can read it fluently.
2. Read all the sentences as a unit.
3. Practise writing each sentence in shorthand until you can write it easily and rapidly.
4. Write all the sentences once as a unit.

Building Dictation Skills

1. Practise writing each sentence from dictation. Keep your text open for easy reference.
2. Read the shorthand you have written in your notebook.
   YOUR AIM: TO WRITE 50 WORDS IN A MINUTE

Reading and Writing Practice

See page 11 for the key to these sentences.

UNIT 4

DEVELOPING TRANSCRIPTION SKILLS

This section of the text and similar sections which follow each lesson
are designed to help you to build your skill in transcribing from your
own shorthand notes to the final typed copy. There are three steps in
the development of transcribing skills.

In the first step you will be asked to type from the printed copy,
not the shorthand. The purpose of this exercise is to give you a
comparison between the time you require to type these sentences from
printed copy and the time you will require to type them from your
shorthand notes. It will also familiarize you with the material you will
be typing from shorthand.

The second step asks you to type from the shorthand in the text.
This step is designed to give you practice in typing material from
perfect shorthand copy. You have read this copy several times and it is
familiar to you. Because it is familiar you will have fewer problems with
this new experience.

The third step has two parts. The material must be dictated to you
so that you can write the shorthand in your own notebook. The next
step is to transcribe this material from your personal shorthand notes.

This plan is designed to develop in three easy stages your ability
to type material directly from your shorthand notes. Of course, your
eventual aim is to transcribe directly from your own shorthand without
going through the first two steps. As you progress through the text each
of the first two steps will gradually disappear.
The following exercises will develop your skill and experience in reading,
writing, and transcribing shorthand.

Transcription from Printed Copy

Transcribe the following sentences on your typewriter. Type easily and
confidently and note especially the punctuation and spelling in each
sentence.

1. I know that the boat is in the bay.[7]
2. I may take you to the game today. I know the name of[10] the
   game.
3. You may take anything you make to the game today.[10]
4. I know the name and the make of the boat that is in the bay.[10]

11

5. You may go to the game today.[6]
6. I came to take you to the boating games in Oak Bay.[10]
7. May I take that boat to go to the games?[7]
8. It may snow today and I may take you to the games.[10]
9. Do you know the date of the games in May?[7]
10. You may stay and you and I may name the boats that go in[10] the bay.

Transcription from Plate Shorthand

From the plate shorthand in the text, transcribe each of the sentences appearing on page 10. It is suggested that you practise the following study plan when transcribing shorthand:

(a) 1. Read the first sentence.
   2. Transcribe the first sentence on your typewriter from the plate shorthand. Read the shorthand as you would when typing from print.
   3. Follow the same plan for each of the other sentences.
(b) 1. Transcribe the whole passage as if it were a paragraph.

Transcription from Dictation

1. Write these sentences in shorthand from dictation.
2. Read your shorthand notes. As you read, insert punctuation
3. From your own notes, transcribe these sentences on your typewriter.
   Try to transcribe fluently and easily with as little hesitation as possible.

4

Writing the sounds of F, V, Th, TH, SES, SEZ, ZEZ; past tense T, D, ED

light ∝ Dark

UNIT 1

Principle Discovery

If the word *foe* is written

If the word *save* is written

If the word *both* is written

If the word *they* is written

If the word *faces* is written

If the word *gazes* is written

can you discover the shorthand signs and principles used in writing the outlines for the words listed below?

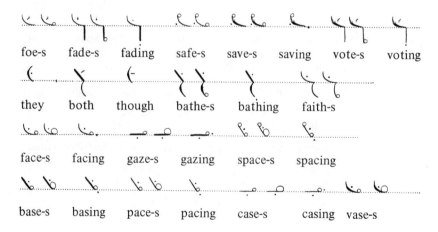

foe-s   fade-s   fading   safe-s   save-s   saving   vote-s   voting

they   both   though   bathe-s   bathing   faith-s

face-s   facing   gaze-s   gazing   space-s   spacing

base-s   basing   pace-s   pacing   case-s   casing   vase-s

Pitman Principles

1. F is a light, curved downstroke as in *foe* and *face*
2. V is a dark, curved downstroke as in *vase* and *save*
3. Th (*ith*) is a light, curved downstroke as in *both* and *faith*
4. TH (*thee*) is a dark, curved downstroke as in *they*
5. S or Z is a small circle as in *face* . A circle double the size represents a double S or Z sound as in *faces* and *gazes* . Be sure to write the SES circle larger than the S circle.
6. Circles are *always* written inside curved strokes as in *face* and *faces* .

Master the outlines in Unit 1 by following Skill-Building Plan 1 on page 9.

UNIT 2

Principle Discovery

Read the following words and discover the principle for writing the past tense sounds T, D, and ED:

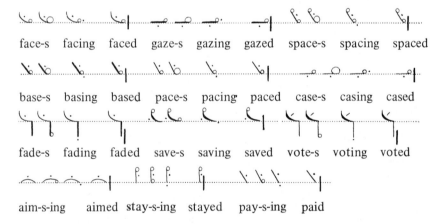

face-s	facing	faced	gaze-s	gazing	gazed	space-s	spacing	spaced
base-s	basing	based	pace-s	pacing	paced	case-s	casing	cased
fade-s	fading	faded	save-s	saving	saved	vote-s	voting	voted

aim-s-ing	aimed stay-s-ing	stayed	pay-s-ing	paid

Pitman Principle

1. The past tense sounds T, D, and ED are shown by a disjoined, straight stroke. The stroke is placed close to the basic outline, as in *faced* .

Master the outlines in Unit 3 by following Skill-Building Plan 1 on page 9.

14

UNIT 3

Pitman Pacers

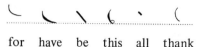

for   have   be   this   all   thank

Phrases

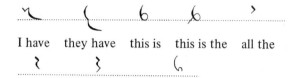

I have   they have   this is   this is the   all the

all that   all that the   thank you

Note: In phrases the S circle is used for *us* and *his*.

to us   for us   of us   to his   for his   of his

Master the outlines in Unit 2 by following Skill-Building Plan 1 on page 9.

UNIT 4

SKILL-BUILDING PLAN 2

Building Reading and Writing Skills

1. Read each sentence until you can read it fluently.
2. Read all the sentences as a unit. Are you reading them without hesitation?
3. Write each sentence in shorthand until you can write it easily and rapidly.
4. Write all the sentences once as a unit.

Building Dictation Skills

1. Write each sentence from dictation. As you write, keep your textbook open for easy reference.
2. Read the shorthand you have written in your notebook.

YOUR AIM: TO WRITE 50 WORDS A MINUTE

15

Reading and Writing Practice

See page 17 for the key to these sentences.

UNIT 5

Developing Transcription Skills

TRANSCRIPTION SKILL-BUILDING PLAN

1. Type the sentences in this Unit. Type easily and confidently and note especially the punctuation and spelling.
2. Transcribe each of the sentences from the plate shorthand in the preceding Unit, using the following method:
   (*a*) Read the sentence.
   (*b*) Transcribe the sentence. As you transcribe, read the shorthand as you do when typing from print.
   (*c*) Transcribe all the sentences as a unit.
3. Write these sentences in shorthand from dictation. Then:
   (*a*) Read your shorthand notes and insert the punctuation.
   (*b*) From your own notes, transcribe these sentences. Aim to transcribe with as little hesitation as possible.

Key to Reading and Writing Practice

1. Is it safe for us to stay in the boat in the bay?[10]
2. May I stay? I stayed for two days.[10]
3. Do you know that I have to go to the games in the same[10] boat?
4. Have you paid for the bait? They have paid for all the bait.[10]
5. Is it safe to have the soap in that case? No, though they[10] aimed to make it safe.
6. This is all the face soap I have. Do you have any?[9]
7. Both you and I voted today. They voted today, too.[10] Thank you for voting.
8. Is it safe for us to bathe in this bay? They have bathed[10] in it. You may stay and bathe in the bay, too.[19]
9. Do you know that all of his tapes may be in that safe? Is[10] that the safe? It may be.[15]
10. I know that it is in the same space. I saved all of[10] that to pay for it.

5 Writing the sound of Y, and vowels Ĕ, Ŭ

UNIT 1

Principle Discovery

If the word *bet* is written ⟍

If the word *up* is written ⟍

If the word *yes* is written ⟋

can you discover the shorthand signs and principles used in writing the outlines for the words listed below?

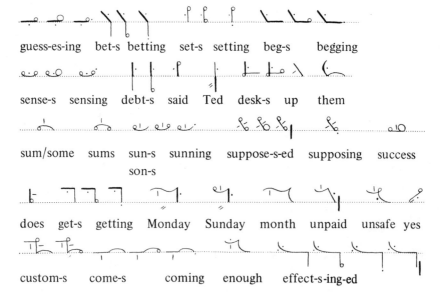

guess-es-ing   bet-s betting   set-s setting   beg-s   begging

sense-s   sensing   debt-s   said   Ted   desk-s   up   them

sum/some   sums   sun-s   sunning   suppose-s-ed   supposing   success
                  son-s

does   get-s   getting   Monday   Sunday   month   unpaid   unsafe yes

custom-s   come-s   coming   enough   effect-s-ing-ed

Pitman Principles

1. The sound Ĕ is shown by a dot as in *bet* ⟍ .
2. The sound Ŭ is shown by a dash as in *up* ⟍ .
3. These vowel signs are written at the middle of the stroke as in *debt* ⌐ and *custom* ⊤⌐ .
4. Write the S circle outside two straight strokes as in *custom* ⊤⌐ and *desk* ⌐ .
5. When a word starts with a horizontal stroke, the first downstroke touches the line as in *get* ⌐ *Monday* ⌐ *Sunday* ⌐ .
6. The sign for Y is ⟋ as in *yes* ⟋ .

> REMEMBER: A dot written at the middle of a stroke always represents the sound of Ĕ or Ā.
> A dash written at the middle of a stroke always represents the sound of Ŭ or Ō.

Master the outlines in Unit 1 by following Skill-Building Plan 1 on page 9.

UNIT 2

Pitman Pacers

yesterday   as/has   but   put

Phrases

In a phrase the ⟍ stroke is used for *hope* as in:

I hope   I hope that   I hope that the   but the   put the   for it

Master the outlines in Unit 2 by following Skill-Building Plan 1 on page 9.

UNIT 3

Reading and Writing Practice

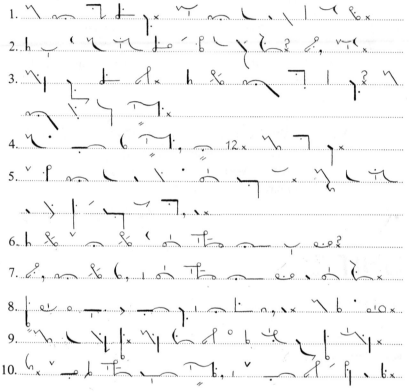

See page 21 for the key to these sentences.

Master the sentences in Unit 3 by following Skill-Building Plan 2 on page 15.

UNIT 4

Developing Transcription Skills

TRANSCRIPTION SKILL-BUILDING PLAN

1. Type the sentences in this Unit. Type easily and confidently and note especially the punctuation and spelling.
2. Transcribe each of the sentences from the plate shorthand in the preceding Unit, using the following method:
    (a) Read the sentence.
    (b) As you transcribe, read the shorthand as you do when typing from print.
    (c) Transcribe all the sentences as a unit.
3. Write these sentences in shorthand from dictation. Then:
    (a) Read your shorthand notes and insert the punctuation.
    (b) From your own notes, transcribe these sentences. Aim to transcribe with as little hesitation as possible.

Key to Reading and Writing Practice

1. I hope you may get the desk today. I know you may have[10] to put it in that space.[14]
2. Do you know that I have enough desks and sets for both of[10] them? Yes, I know that.[14]
3. I hoped to take the desk yesterday. Do you suppose you[10] may be getting it today? I hope you may be paying[20] for it Monday.[23]
4. I have a game this Monday, May 12. I hope you get to[10] it.
5. I said you may have to pay a sum to get in. I hope[10] that you have enough to pay the debt and to get in the[20] gate, too.
6. Do you suppose I may suppose that some customs make no[10] sense?
7. Yes, you may suppose this, but some customs make sense to some[10] of them.[11]
8. Ted's son is going to the game today but may take you,[10] too. I hope it is a success.[16]
9. I hope you have paid the debts. I paid them yesterday as[10] it is unsafe to have the debts unpaid.[17]
10. Thank you. I guess it is the custom to come Mondays, but[10] I came yesterday and stayed two days.[17]

6 Writing the sounds of L, W, NG

UNIT 1

Principle Discovery

If the word *low* is written _⌐_
If the word *weigh* is written _⌐_
If the word *sung* is written _ᴗ_

can you discover the shorthand signs and principles used in writing
the outlines for the words listed below?

low	load-s-ing-ed	lay-s-ing/laid	love-s	loving	loved

lake-s	less	led	leg-s	else	sail-s-ing	sailed
					sale-s	

self	selfless	slow-s-ing-ed	below	delay-s-ing-ed

detail-s-ing-ed	mail-s-ing-ed	weigh-s-ing-ed
		way-s

22

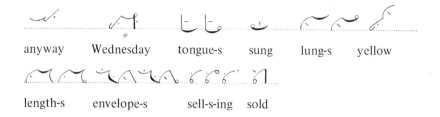

anyway	Wednesday	tongue-s	sung	lung-s	yellow

length-s	envelope-s	sell-s-ing	sold

Pitman Principles

1. L is a light, curved stroke written upward as in *low*
2. W is a light, straight upstroke with a hook at the beginning as in *way*
3. NG is a dark stroke as in *sung*

Master the outlines in Unit 1 by following Skill-Building Plan 1 on page 9.

UNIT 2

Pacers and Phrases

The Pitman Pacer for *will* is and for *we* is

1. In a phrase, the stroke is used for *will* as in:

you will	you will be	you will be the	it will	it will be

it will be the	they will	they will be	you will have

2. In a phrase, the stroke is used for *we* as in:

we have	we have the	we will	we will be

we hope	we hope that	we hope that the

Master the phrases in Unit 2 by following Skill-Building Plan 1 on page 9.

UNIT 3

Reading and Writing Practice

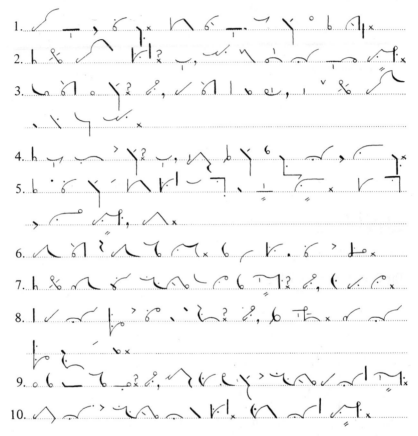

See page 25 for the key to these sentences.

Master the sentences in Unit 3 by following Skill-Building Plan 2 on page 15.

UNIT 4

Developing Transcription Skills

Develop your transcribing skills by following the Transcription Skill-Building Plan on page 21.

24

Key to Reading and Writing Practice

1. We will go to the sale today. It will be slow going[10] in the boat as it is loaded.[15]
2. Do you suppose we will be delayed? No, anyway I[10] hope some mail comes Wednesday.[14]
3. Have you sold his boat? Yes, we sold it to his son, but I[10] suppose we will have to pay for it anyway.[17]
4. Do you know the name of the boat? No, but we hope that it[10] is the boat that is to take the mail to the lake today.[20]
5. It is a sail boat and it will be delayed in getting[10] to Oak Lake. It will get to the lakes Wednesday, we hope.[20]
6. We have sold all that we have in this length. This will delay[10] the sale of the desks.[13]
7. Do you suppose you will have to sell the envelopes for[10] less this Monday? Yes, they weigh less.[15]
8. Do we mail the details of the sales to all of them? Yes,[10] this is the custom. You will mail the details to them and[20] to us.
9. Is this to go in this case? Yes, and we hope that they will[10] save both of the envelopes we mailed Monday.[19]
10. We hope the mailing of the envelopes may be delayed.[10] They will be mailed Wednesday.[16]

7 Writing the sounds of R, INGS

UNIT 1

Pitman Principles

1. There are two ways to write the sound of R: upward R and downward R
2. Upward R begins a word as in *ray*
3. Downward R ends a word as in *door*
4. Upward R is used in the middle of a word as in *purpose*
5. Downward R is *always* used before M as in *roam*
6. A dot written at the end of a word represents the sound of ING. A small dash written at the end of a word represents the sound of INGS.

These principles are shown in the words given below:

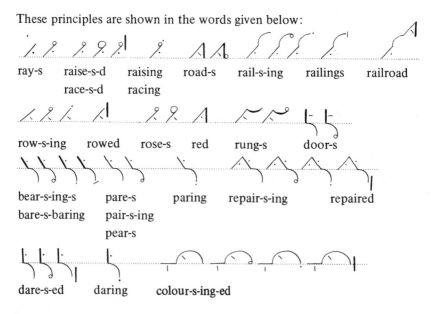

ray-s   raise-s-d   raising   road-s   rail-s-ing   railings   railroad
       race-s-d   racing

row-s-ing   rowed   rose-s   red   rung-s   door-s

bear-s-ing-s   pare-s   paring   repair-s-ing   repaired
bare-s-baring   pair-s-ing
           pear-s

dare-s-ed   daring   colour-s-ing-ed

26

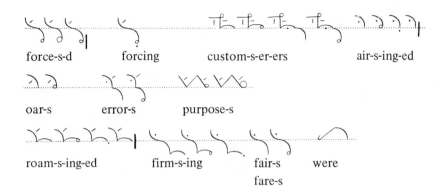

force-s-d   forcing   custom-s-er-ers   air-s-ing-ed

oar-s   error-s   purpose-s

roam-s-ing-ed   firm-s-ing   fair-s   were
                               fare-s

Note: When a vowel begins a word, use downward R ⟍ as in:

error *but* rare

When a vowel ends a word, use upward R ╱ as in:

burrow *but* burr

SKILL-BUILDING PLAN 1

Reading and Writing Practice

1. Read the shorthand outlines in this Unit, preferably repeating the words out loud.
2. Cover the printed words and read the shorthand outlines.
3. Write the shorthand outlines in your notebook until you can write them quickly and confidently.
4. Write the shorthand outlines from dictation. Keep your text open as you write. Refer to your text for assistance whenever necessary.
5. Read the shorthand which you have taken from dictation.

YOUR AIM: TO WRITE 50 WORDS A MINUTE

UNIT 2

Pitman Pacers

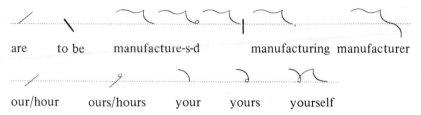

are	to be	manufacture-s-d		manufacturing	manufacturer

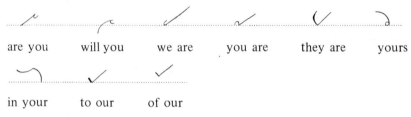

our/hour	ours/hours	your	yours	yourself

Phrases

Note: In some phrases YOU is turned for easier writing.

are you	will you	we are	you are	they are	yours

in your	to our	of our

Master Unit 2 by following Skill-Building Plan 1 on page 27.

UNIT 3

Reading and Writing Practice

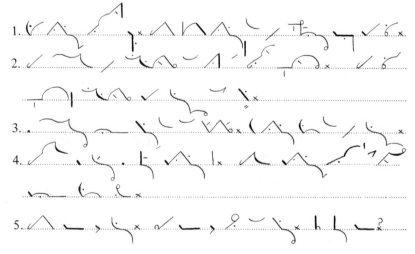

WRITING TIP: Write // to indicate a paragraph.
See page 30 for the key to this Unit.

SKILL-BUILDING PLAN 2

Building Reading and Writing Skills

1. Read each sentence until you can read it fluently.
2. Read all the sentences as a unit. Are you reading them without hesitation?
3. Practise writing each sentence in shorthand until you can write it easily and rapidly.
4. Write all the sentences once as a unit.

Building Dictation Skills

1. Practise writing each sentence from dictation. Keep your text open for easy reference.
2. Read the shorthand you have written in your notebook.

Note: When you have finished practising the sentences, follow the same plan in studying the paragraph.

YOUR AIM: TO WRITE 50 WORDS A MINUTE

UNIT 4

1. Type the sentences in this Unit. Type easily and confidently and note especially the punctuation and spelling.
2. Transcribe each of the sentences from the plate shorthand in the preceding Unit using the following method:
   (a) Read each sentence.
   (b) As you transcribe, read the shorthand as you do when typing from print.
   (c) Transcribe all the sentences as a unit.
3. Write these sentences in shorthand from dictation. Then:
   (a) Read your shorthand notes and insert the punctuation.
   (b) From your own notes, transcribe these sentences.
       Aim to transcribe with as little hesitation as possible.
4. Follow the above plan when transcribing the paragraph.

Key to Reading and Writing Practice

1. They will repair the railroad today. We hope it will be[10] repaired for our customers to get to our sale.[20]
2. **We manufacture our envelopes in red and yellow**[10] colours. We sell the colored envelopes to our firms in[20] the Bay.
3. The manufacturers make bearings for any purpose.[10] They repair them for our firm.[15]
4. We will have to force the door to repair it. We have to[10] repair the railings and the rungs to make them safe.[19]
5. We hope to go to the fair You are to go to the races[10] in pairs. Do you dare to go?[15]
6. The custom is fair, but its purpose is to force the firms[10] to pay for the repairs.[15]

7. Memo to Ted Dare:

The purposes of our firm's sale for[10] the month of May were detailed to you yesterday. I hope[20] you are going to be a customer of ours. We are[30] manufacturing for our firm's customers, and we hope[40] for you, coloured road sets for all roads and railroads.

Do you[50] care enough to come to the sale?

Yours,
The Roller Bearings[60] Firm

8 Halving strokes

UNIT 1

Principle Discovery

If the word *coat* is written ....⊤....
If the word *left* is written ...⌐⌐...
If the word *bed* is written ...⟍...

can you discover the shorthand signs and principles used in writing the outlines for the words listed below?

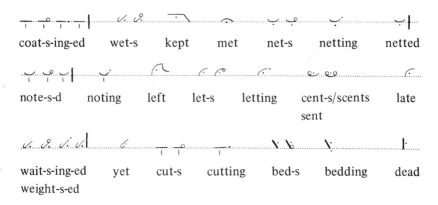

coat-s-ing-ed   wet-s   kept   met   net-s   netting   netted

note-s-d   noting   left   let-s   letting   cent-s/scents sent   late

wait-s-ing-ed   yet   cut-s   cutting   bed-s   bedding   dead
weight-s-ed

Pitman Principles

1. In one-syllable words, light strokes are halved to indicate a following sound of T. *light for a light*
2. In one-syllable words, dark strokes are halved to indicate a following sound of D. *Dark for a Dark.*

Master the outlines in Unit 1 by following Skill-Building Plan 1 on page 27.

32

UNIT 2

Principle Discovery

If the word *method* is written ⟋
If the word *result* is written ⟋
If the word *report* is written ⟋
If the word *certain* is written ⟋

can you discover the shorthand signs and principles used to write the
outlines for the words listed below?

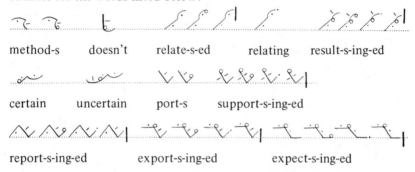

method-s	doesn't	relate-s-ed	relating	result-s-ing-ed

certain	uncertain	port-s	support-s-ing-ed

report-s-ing-ed	export-s-ing-ed	expect-s-ing-ed

Pitman Principles

1. In words of more than one syllable a stroke is halved to indicate a following sound of T or D.
2. Half-length upward R is generally used to express the sound of RT.

Master the outlines in Unit 2 by following Skill-Building Plan 1 on page 27.

UNIT 3

Phrases

Were is written ⟋ . In phrases, *were* may be written ⟋ as in:

we were	they were	you were	were you

Master Unit 3 by following Skill-Building Plan 1 on page 27.

33

UNIT 4

Reading and Writing Practice

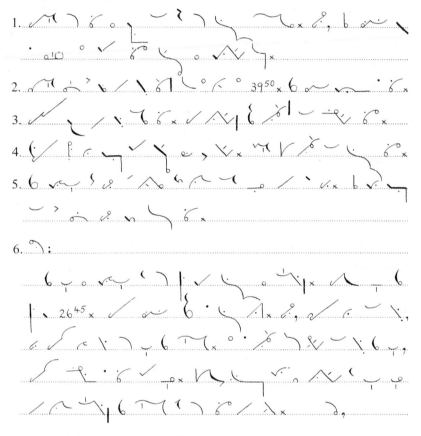

See page 35 for the key to this Unit.

Master Unit 4 by following Skill-Building Plan 2 on page 29.

UNIT 5

Developing Transcription Skills

Develop your transcribing skills by following the Transcription Skill-Building Plan on page 30.

Key to Reading and Writing Practice

1. We note that your sale is to take in all that your firm[10] manufactures. Yes, it is certain to be a success as[20] all our sales force is to report for it.[27]

2. You will note that some of the beds are being sold for as[10] low as $39.50. This is certain to[20] make a sale.

3. We were to have our bedding in this sale. We reported[10] that this resulted in export sales.[17]

4. They were staying late to get all our boats sent to the port.[10] I note that it will result in fairer sales.[17]

5. This is to let you know that the weights and ropes that you left[10] in that case are all wet. It is too late to get any[20] of the same weights to you for your sale.[27]

6. Sir:

    This note is to let you know that your debt to our firm[10] is unpaid. We have cut this debt to $26.45.[20] We are certain that this is a fair rate. Yes, you were late[30] in paying, yet we will let you pay your note this month. As[40] a result of your support in paying this note, we will[50] expect a sale of our coats. It will have the effect of[60] letting you report that no notes are left unpaid this month[70] and that your sales are up.

    Yours,[75]

9

Writing the sounds of CH, J, S and Z, SH, and ZH

Unit 1

Principle Discovery

If the word *check* is written ___/___

If the word *age* is written ___/___

If the word *us* is written ___)___

If the word *owes* is written ___)___

If the word *show* is written ___/___

can you discover the shorthand signs and principles used in writing the outlines for the words listed below?

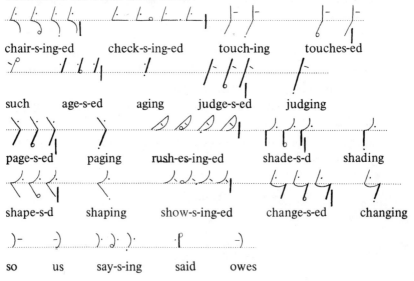

chair-s-ing-ed   check-s-ing-ed   touch-ing   touches-ed

such   age-s-ed   aging   judge-s-ed   judging

page-s-ed   paging   rush-es-ing-ed   shade-s-d   shading

shape-s-d   shaping   show-s-ing-ed   change-s-ed   changing

so   us   say-s-ing   said   owes

Pitman Principles

1. CH is a light downstroke as in *check* _⌐_. J is a dark downstroke as in *age* _⌐_.
2. SH and ZH is a light, curved downstroke as in *show* _⌐_.
3. A curved downstroke represents the sound of S and Z and is used in words like *us* _⌐_ and *owes* _⌐_. In such outlines the stroke is used instead of the circle, so that the vowel sign can be placed.

Master the outlines in Unit 1 by following Skill-Building Plan 1 on page 27.

Unit 2

Pitman Pacers

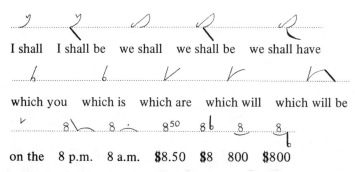

shall   which   on   had/dollar

Phrases

I shall   I shall be   we shall   we shall be   we shall have

which you   which is   which are   which will   which will be

on the   8 p.m.   8 a.m. $8.50 $8   800 $800

Master Unit 2 by following Skill-Building Plan 1 on page 27.

Unit 3

Reading and Writing Practice

See page 39 for the key to this Unit.

Master Unit 3 by following Skill-Building Plan 2 on page 29.

Unit 4

Developing Transcription Skills

Develop your transcribing skills by following the Transcription Skill-Building Plan on page 30.

Key to Reading and Writing Practice

1. We shall be in the show and I shall be waiting for you[10] and for them. I checked it, and the show is 8 p.m., Monday.[20]

2. I hope they will make no changes in the show. Yes, I checked[10] it for changes yesterday and I judge they will make some.[20]

3. Show us which are the chairs you will be showing in the fair.[10] We shall take some of the yellow chairs.[17]

4. We have checked all the pages which we have. You will have to touch[10] up some of them to make certain they make sense to us.[20]

5. Joe owes a debt of $1,200. We shall have to[10] take this to Judge Rose to force Joe to pay us.[17]

6. The manufacturer of the 800 yellow shades[10] said that they will rush repairs so that we may have them for[20] the show.

7. This yellow page is the shape and length we said we were[10] going to cut. Thank you for cutting all the pages so that[20] they were the same length.

8. James Rose:

   This is to let you know that on Wednesday we[10] are having a sale of chairs and desks which are slow sellers.[20] It is an error for us to manufacture them in[30] such a way that they are certain to have a slow sale. As[40] you were a customer of ours, we hope you will come to this[50] sale.

   Stay in touch in case we have some changes in the[60] sale.

   Yours,

10 Writing the sounds of PL, BL, TL, DL, KL, GL

Unit 1

Principle Discovery

If the word *play* is written ⟍

If the word *able* is written ⟍

If the word *close* is written ⌒ₒ

If the word *settle* is written ⌐

can you discover the shorthand signs and principles used in writing the outlines for the words listed below?

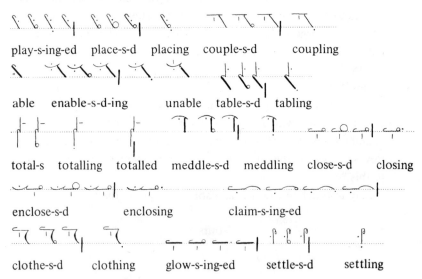

play-s-ing-ed   place-s-d   placing   couple-s-d   coupling

able   enable-s-d-ing   unable   table-s-d   tabling

total-s   totalling   totalled   meddle-s-d   meddling   close-s-d   closing

enclose-s-d   enclosing   claim-s-ing-ed

clothe-s-d   clothing   glow-s-ing-ed   settle-s-d   settling

40

Pitman Principles

1. A small hook at the beginning of a straight stroke adds the sound of L. To express the double consonant sounds PL, BL, TL, DL, KL, GL, write the small hook on the same side of the stroke as the S circle.

2. To express S plus a double consonant sound, ⟍⟍ etc., write the S circle inside the hook as in *settle* ⟍

written on the Right
it written on the same
as a S. Circle

SKILL-BUILDING PLAN 1

Reading and Writing Practice

1. Read the shorthand outlines in this Unit, preferably reading the words out loud.
2. Cover the printed words and read the shorthand outlines.
3. Write the shorthand outlines in your notebook until you can write them easily and quickly.
4. Write the shorthand outlines from dictation. Keep your text open as you write. Refer to your text for assistance whenever necessary.
5. Read the shorthand which you have taken from dictation.

YOUR AIM: TO WRITE 50 WORDS A MINUTE

Unit 2

Pitman Pacers

who   large   largely   able to

Phrases

who will   who will be   who are   to be able to

As a speed device, ‿ can be shortened in phrases:

I will   I will be   I will have   I may   I may have   you will be able to

Master the outlines in Unit 2 by following Skill-Building Plan 1 above.

Unit 3

SKILL-BUILDING PLAN 2

Building Reading and Writing Skills

1. Read each sentence until you can read it fluently.
2. Read all the sentences as a unit. Are you reading them without hesitation?
3. Practise writing each sentence in shorthand until you can write it easily and rapidly.
4. Write all the sentences once as a unit.

Building Dictation Skills

1. Practise writing each sentence from dictation. Keep your text open for easy reference.
2. Read the shorthand you have written in your notebook.
3. When you have completed the sentences, follow the same plan to practise the letter.

    YOUR AIM: TO WRITE 60 WORDS A MINUTE

Reading and Writing Practice

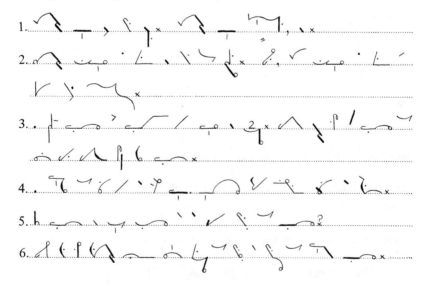

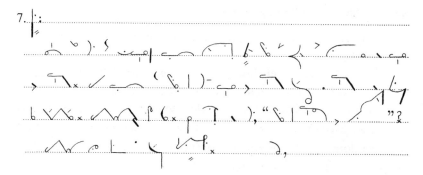

7.

See page 44 for the key to this Unit.

Unit 4

Developing Transcription Skills

Up to this point three steps have been followed in the development of the transcription skill. In this plan it is suggested that Step 1 be dropped and that transcription should begin directly from the plate shorthand in the text. If, however, you find that transcribing directly from plate shorthand causes you undue difficulty, continue the three-step plan for several more lessons. The point at which Step 1 should be dropped is a matter of individual judgement.

TRANSCRIPTION SKILL-BUILDING PLAN

1. Transcribe the sentences from the plate shorthand in the preceding Unit, using the following method:
    (a) Read each sentence.
    (b) Transcribe each sentence. As you transcribe, read the shorthand as you read when typing from print.
    (c) Transcribe all the sentences as a unit.
2. Write these sentences in shorthand from dictation. Then:
    (a) Read your shorthand notes and insert the punctuation. If you are not sure of the spelling of a word, check it in your dictionary before you begin to transcribe.
    (b) From your own notes, transcribe these sentences.
3. Follow the above plan when transcribing the letter.

Key to Reading and Writing Practice

1. I will be able to go to the play today. I will[10] be able to go on Monday, too.[17]

2. You will be able to enclose a cheque to pay for the[10] tables. Yes, I will enclose a cheque and it will pay the[20] manufacturer.

3. The total claims of the clerk are close to $200.[10] We hope to be able to settle large claims in the[20] same way we have settled this claim.[26]

4. The clothes in the sale are all of such glowing colours that[10] we expect to sell all of them.[16]

5. Do you claim to know the names of all who are playing in[10] the games?

6. Yesterday they said they will be able to make some changes[10] in the placing of players in the club games.[18]

7. Ted:

    Some of us say that the enclosed claim locating Joe's[10] place on the shore of the lake is too close to the club. We[20] claim that placing it so close to the club forces the club[30] to change its purpose. We hope you will be able to settle[40] this. Is it meddling to say, "Place it closer to the[50] railroad"?

    We hope you will let us take a vote on[60] Wednesday.

    Yours,

11

Writing the sounds of Ă, AH; Ŏ, AW

UNIT 1

Principle Discovery

If the word *at* is written ⌐

If the word *cash* is written ⌐

can you discover the shorthand signs and principles used in writing the outlines for the words listed below?

am	at	add-s-ing-ed	bag-s	bagging-ed	baggage

pass-es-ing-ed	act-s-ing-ed	away	ago

await-s-ing-ed	bank-s-ing-ed	back-s-ing-ed

tax-es-ing-ed	cash-es-ing-ed	sample-s-d	sampling

start-s-ing-ed	ask-s-ing-ed	car-s

Pitman Principles

the a and Ah are represented by dot.

1. The sounds Ă and AH are represented by a dot written at the beginning of a stroke as in *at* ⌐ and *car* ⌐.

written at the beginning of a stroke as in at in a car

46

2. The first up or downstroke does not touch the line as in:

   add ____ *away* ____ *bag* ____ *baggage* ____ .

3. *Note*: It is the first vowel sound in a word which is important.
   If the first vowel sound is Ă or AH, write the first up or downstroke
   above the line as in *sample* ____ . This is known as *first position.*
   Contrast *sample* ____ and *example* ____ .

Master the outlines in Unit 1 by following Skill-Building Plan 1 on
page 41.

UNIT 2

Principle Discovery

Read the following words and discover the signs and principles for writing
the sounds of Ŏ and AW:

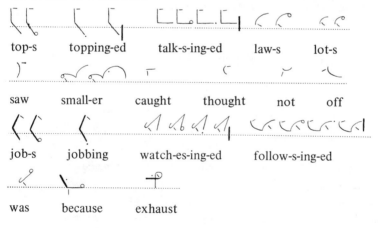

| top-s | topping-ed | talk-s-ing-ed | law-s | lot-s |

| saw | small-er | caught | thought | not | off |

| job-s | jobbing | watch-es-ing-ed | follow-s-ing-ed |

| was | because | exhaust |

Pitman Principles

1. The sounds of Ŏ and AW are represented by a dash written at the
   beginning of a stroke as in:

   talk ____ and *law* ____ .

2. The first up or downstroke does not touch the line as in:

   raw ⟋ and *follow* ⟍⟋.

3. *Note*: It is the first vowel sound in a word which is important. If the first vowel sound is Ŏ or AW, write the first up or downstroke above the line as in *follow* ⟍⟋ . This is known as *first position*. Contrast *follow* ⟍⟋ and *fellow* ⟍⟋ .

4. Vowel sounds other than Ĕ may be used with the SES circle. The vowel is placed inside the circle as in *exhaust* ⟋⟋ .

Master the outlines in Unit 2 by following Skill-Building Plan 1 on page 41.

UNIT 3

Building Vocabulary Skills

The following words are all written in first position:

charge-s-d   charging   March   mark-s-ing-ed

garage-s   park-s-ing-ed   march-es-ing-ed

market-s-ing-ed   long-s-ing-ed   box-es-ing-ed

catalogue-s-d   cataloguing   cause-s-d   causing   wrong-s-ed

shop-s   shopping-ed   cargo-s

Master the outlines in Unit 3 by following Skill-Building Plan 1 on page 41.

48

UNIT 4

Reading and Writing Practice

See page 50 for the key to these sentences.

Master Unit 4 by following Skill-Building Plan 2 on page 42.

UNIT 5

Developing Transcription Skills

To develop your transcribing skill further, follow the Transcription Skill-Building Plan on page 43.

Key to Reading and Writing Practice

1. We will be away for the month of March and we will not[10] be able to go to the shops at the fair in the market[20] place.
2. We hope that they will market the watches that were in the[10] catalogue on Monday. I hope that they will be showing[20] the sample lots on Sunday.
3. We will be watching the results of the boxing match. This[10] match has caused some cars to be charged for parking in the market[20] parking lot.
4. We are unable to cash our cheques at the bank. We have to[10] have the cash for shopping.
5. The market was off to a bad start today. Some board lots[10] are being sold. Have you any cash in the market? No,[20] I have exhausted all our cash long ago.
6. I had a small percentage of savings in the market.[10] They aided us in paying taxes.
7. The packages are in the car. I will ask Jack to take[10] the car to the parking lot at the back of the bank.[20]
8. I thought I had the samples in the packages, but they[10] had the samples in the top of that small box in the[20] garage in the park.
9. I will pass the cash to you at the start of the game. Put[10] it in the back of your car and take it away to the bank.[20]
10. We shall have samples of the cargo sent to you. You saw[10] that some of the boxes in the cargo had the wrong tops[20] on them. Let us know your thoughts on the sale of this cargo.[30]

12

Writing the sounds of Ī and OI

UNIT 1

Principle Discovery

If the word *by* is written

If the word *mile* is written

If the word *advise* is written

If the word *item* is written

can you discover the shorthand signs and principles used in writing the outlines for the words listed below?

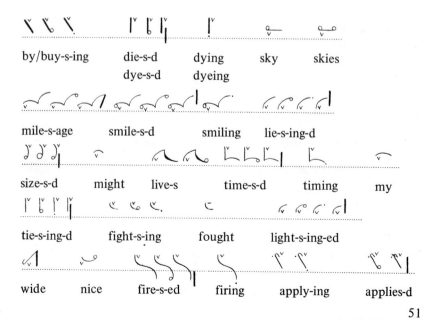

by/buy-s-ing	die-s-d	dying	sky	skies
	dye-s-d	dyeing		

mile-s-age   smile-s-d   smiling   lie-s-ing-d

size-s-d	might	live-s	time-s-d	timing	my

tie-s-ing-d   fight-s-ing   fought   light-s-ing-ed

wide	nice	fire-s-ed	firing	apply-ing	applies-d

51

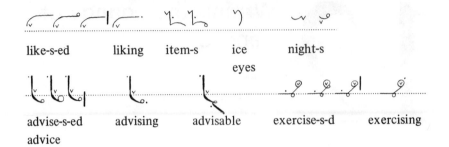

like-s-ed	liking	item-s	ice	night-s
			eyes	

advise-s-ed	advising	advisable	exercise-s-d	exercising
advice				

Pitman Principles

1. The sound Ī is represented by the sign ⌄ written at the beginning of a stroke, as in *by* ⟍ and *time* ⌐.
2. When I is the first vowel sound in a word, the first up or downstroke is written in first position above the line as in *wide* ⟋| and *fire* ⟍.
3. The sign for I may be joined in words such as *item* ⌐ and *eyes* ⟩.
4. Stroke S is written when initial S is followed by S or Z as in: *size* ⟩ and *sizes* ∂.

Master Unit 1 by following Skill-Building Plan 1 on page 41.

UNIT 2

Principle Discovery

If the word *boy* is written ⟍

If the word *voice* is written ⟍₀

If the word *enjoy* is written ⟍⌐

If the word *employer* is written ⟍⤳ *any test I don't have*

If the word *buyer* is written ⟍ *to put it in.*

can you discover the shorthand signs and principles used in writing the outlines for the words listed below?

boy-s	joy-s	soil-s-ing-ed	voice-s-ed	voicing

52

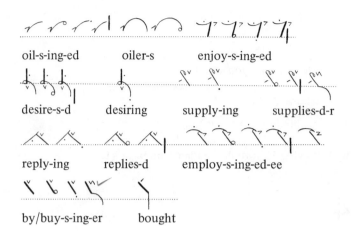

oil-s-ing-ed   oiler-s   enjoy-s-ing-ed

desire-s-d   desiring   supply-ing   supplies-d-r

reply-ing   replies-d   employ-s-ing-ed-ee

by/buy-s-ing-er   bought

Pitman Principles

1. The sound OI is represented by the sign ⌐ written at the beginning of a stroke.

2. When OI is the first vowel sound in a word, the first up or down-stroke is written in first position above the line as in *boy* ⌐ and *soil* ⌐ .

3. The first vowel sound in a word determines its position as in *enjoy* ⌐ and *desire* ⌐ .

4. A small tick added to the Ī and OI signs indicates a following vowel sound as in *employee* ⌐ and *buyer* ⌐ .
   This additional sign is used to help to make transcription more rapid and accurate.

Master Unit 2 by following Skill-Building Plan 1 on page 41.

UNIT 3

Pitman Pacers

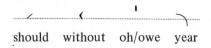

should   without   oh/owe   year

Phrases

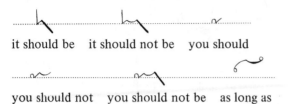

it should be   it should not be   you should

you should not   you should not be   as long as

Master Unit 3 by following Skill-Building Plan 1 on page 41.

UNIT 4

Reading and Writing Practice

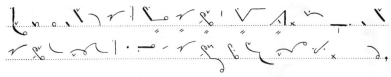

See below for the key to this Unit.

Master Unit 4 by following Skill-Building Plan 2 on page 42.

UNIT 5

Developing Transcription Skill

To develop your transcribing skill, follow the Transcription Skill-Building Plan on page 43.

Key to Reading and Writing Practice

1. You are wise to buy the items that you like without waiting,[10] as long as you know they are the right size for you.[20]
2. Have you checked to make certain the cloth does not soil? The[10] manufacturer says that it should be all right.[19]
3. In your reply, be certain to advise the bank of all[10] the facts of the sale. The sale of oil may be advisable,[20] but the bank should know all that is taking place.[28]
4. We shall be delighted to supply all the items you desire.[10] Let us know the size, colour, and shape you like. We know that[20] your employers should enjoy them.[25]
5. Without some of the employers and employees to aid[10] you, you are wise not to fight the fire. In this way, you may[20] be able to save some lives.[25]
6. Roy:

    I am late in replying to your note of March 17[10] because we have had a bad fire in the oil supplies. We[20] have had a total loss of oil supplies. We saw the light[30] of the fire in the night sky. At times, the smoke and fire rose[40] a mile in the sky. My employer and some of his[50] employees fought the fire all night long. The blaze became too[60] large for any of them to fight it.

    My advice to you[70] is to buy your oil at Black's Oil Supplies on Park Road. I am[80] going to buy oil supplies for myself at a gas[90] and oil supplier's place five miles away. Yours,[98]

13

Writing the sounds of ST and STER; MD and ND

UNIT 1

Principle Discovery

If the word *must* is written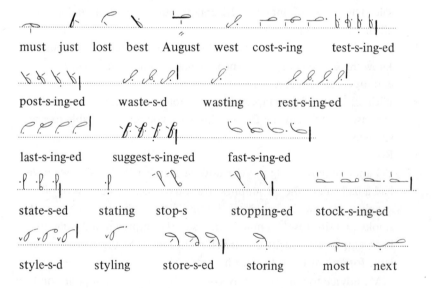

If the word *test* is written

If the word *style* is written

If the word *rests* is written

can you discover the shorthand signs and principles used in writing the outlines for the words listed below?

must   just   lost   best   August   west   cost-s-ing   test-s-ing-ed

post-s-ing-ed   waste-s-d   wasting   rest-s-ing-ed

last-s-ing-ed   suggest-s-ing-ed   fast-s-ing-ed

state-s-ed   stating   stop-s   stopping-ed   stock-s-ing-ed

style-s-d   styling   store-s-ed   storing   most   next

Pitman Principles

1. A small loop represents the sound of ST.
2. The loop for ST can be written at the beginning, in the middle, or at the end of a word.
3. Note how the sound of S is written following ST.

Master Unit 1 by following Skill-Building Plan 1 on page 41.

UNIT 2

Pitman Principles

1. A large loop in the middle or at the end of a word expresses the sound of STER.

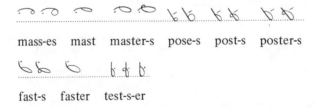

master-s-ing-ed   foster-s-ing-ed   poster-s

2. All these loops are developed from the S circle:

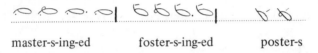

mass-es   mast   master-s   pose-s   post-s   poster-s

fast-s   faster   test-s-er

Note how the sound of S is written following STER.

3. Halved M is darkened to add the sound of D as in *made* and *mad* .
   Halved N is darkened to add the sound of D as in *end* and *send* .

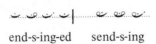

end-s-ing-ed   send-s-ing

Master Unit 2 by following Skill-Building Plan 1 on page 41.

57

UNIT 3

Pitman Pacers

influence   influenced   largest   would   several

Phrases

would be   I would be   I would not be   we would   we would be

we would not be   they would   they would be   they would not be

would you   it would be   it would be the   for several

Master Unit 3 by following Skill-Building Plan 1 on page 41.

UNIT 4

Reading and Writing Practice

58

See below for the key to this Unit.

Master Unit 4, by following Skill-Building Plan 2 on page 42.

UNIT 5

Developing Transcription Skills

To develop skill in transcribing from shorthand, follow the Transcription Skill-Building Plan given on page 43.

Key to Reading and Writing Practice

1. In the end, we must all pay taxes on anything we[10] made last year. It is best to pay our taxes by August[20] 31. You must state that your taxes are based on[30] the stock in your store on the last day of the month.[39]

2. I like the styles and the stock in that store we saw on West[10] Road. I would suggest that we go back and buy several[20] of the best items in the stock.[26]

3. I suggest that it would not be wise to buy for the rest[10] of this month. We are testing the market and a fast fall[20] in the stock market would not be unexpected. The[30] faster the fall, the faster our losses must rise.[39]

4. I would suggest that this is the best time to buy posters.[10] Costs for posters are low. The cost of well-styled posters[20] should rise faster next month. I suggest you should buy the[30] coloured posters.

5. To Our Charge Customers:

    Our store decided to have its[10] style show for its charge customers last March. This style show lasted[20] four days, just long enough for most of you to enjoy[30] it without being rushed.

    Customers who saw the show at[40] that time suggested that a show in August would be best[50] for this year. The enclosed blank form is our way of checking[60] your desires. Would you like a sale in August?

    May we[70] have your reply?

                                          Yours,

                                                              59

OMITTING VOWELS

In longhand, vowels are frequently omitted as a means of shortening words. For instance, *Pd.* stands for *paid* and *Rd.* stands for *road*. The majority of the words in the English language can be read easily when only the consonants are written. In *Pitman Shorterhand* all the sounded consonants are written –except, in the case of the contracted forms which we know as Pacers. These outlines are so distinctive that they can be read as easily as longhand even when written without the vowels. When writing shorthand it is usually unnecessary to insert the vowel signs because the consonant structure is all that is required to make the outline easily transcribable.

In *Pitman Shorterhand* vowels may be inserted or omitted as desired. Omitting a vowel sign does not affect the consonantal structure of the outline, and for this reason outlines can still be read quickly and easily. It is this quality of the system–the ability to insert or drop vowels as desired–that enables Pitman writers to take dictation at much higher speeds than would be possible if the vowels had to be inserted. However, when the writer feels that the insertion of a vowel will help transcription speed, it is possible to drop them in easily and quickly. You know that the first vowel in a word determines the position in which an outline is written. Therefore, correct positioning of outlines immediately identifies the first vowel sound even when the sign has been omitted.

WRITING VOWELS

When should vowels be inserted in your shorthand notes? The answer depends very largely upon the rate of dictation. If the dictation is fast, make an effort to insert vowels which you feel are necessary for rapid transcription, but be sure to write the consonant outlines for every word. Usually the first vowel in the word is important. Never spend time inserting vowels if by doing so you are likely to omit words in your notes. Experience will be your best teacher in this aspect of your shorthand writing. The insertion of as many vowels as possible in the early stages of your speed development work will give you added confidence when transcribing. As a general rule, the longer the outline the more distinctive it is; consequently, the less important the vowels become. One-syllable words, especially those with a beginning vowel, are read more rapidly and more easily when a vowel is inserted.

Remember: when you must choose between inserting vowel signs and getting down outlines for all of the dictation, it is better to write the outlines without the vowels. Context will help you to transcribe outlines in which only the consonants are written, but nothing will help you to transcribe material in which only half the outlines have been written, even though in these outlines all the vowels have been inserted.

When writing shorthand from fast dictation, put the vowels in only when you have time to do so, or if you feel a particular word is unfamiliar and may cause difficulty. Read your notes over immediately after dictation, or as soon as you have an opportunity to do so. This is the time to insert vowels as you read in order to make the transcription as easy as possible.

If you have difficulty reading a particular word do not spend too much time trying to decipher it; read the rest of the sentence, then reread the words coming before the outline causing difficulty. The context, or the sense of the sentence, plus your shorthand outline and your knowledge of English will tell you what the outline represents.

Now continue with your study of *Pitman Shorterhand,* writing it confidently by making full use of the system's flexibility, readability, and dependability for fast transcription.

14

Writing the sounds of the double consonants PR, BR, TR, DR, CHR, JR, KR, GR

UNIT 1

Pitman Principles

1. A small hook on the side of straight strokes opposite to the S circle adds the sound of R.

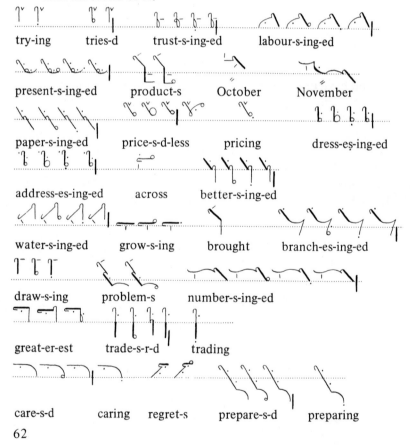

try-ing   tries-d   trust-s-ing-ed   labour-s-ing-ed

present-s-ing-ed   product-s   October   November

paper-s-ing-ed   price-s-d-less   pricing   dress-es-ing-ed

address-es-ing-ed   across   better-s-ing-ed

water-s-ing-ed   grow-s-ing   brought   branch-es-ing-ed

draw-s-ing   problem-s   number-s-ing-ed

great-er-est   trade-s-r-d   trading

care-s-d   caring   regret-s   prepare-s-d   preparing

2. When a lightly sounded vowel occurs between the consonant and the sound of R, we omit the vowel as in:

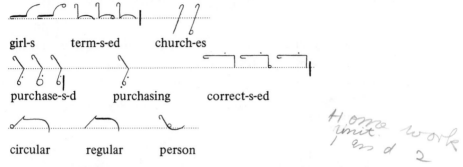

girl-s   term-s-ed   church-es

purchase-s-d   purchasing   correct-s-ed

circular   regular   person

3. To get shorter and more easily written outlines for a few common words the hooked signs are sometimes used even when a strongly sounded vowel comes between the double consonants as in:

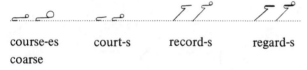

course-es   court-s   record-s   regard-s
coarse

Master Unit 1 by following Skill-Building Plan 1 on page 41.

UNIT 2

Pitman Pacers

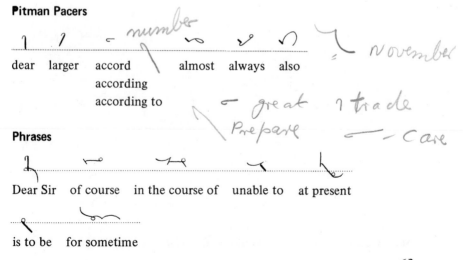

dear   larger   accord   almost   always   also
                according
                according to

Phrases

Dear Sir   of course   in the course of   unable to   at present

is to be   for sometime

Note: When convenient, intersect stroke K  for the word *company* as in:

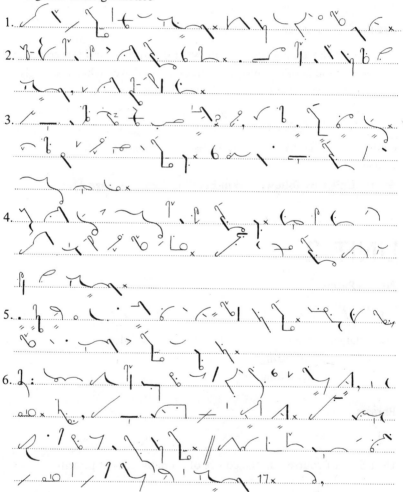

this company   your company   our company   manufacturing company

Master Unit 2 by following Skill-Building Plan 2 on page 41.

UNIT 3
Reading and Writing Practice

See page 65 for the key to this Unit.

Master Unit 3 by following Skill-Building Plan 2 on page 42.

UNIT 4

Developing Transcription Skills

To develop your transcription skills, follow the Transcription Skill-Building Plan on page 43.

Key to Reading and Writing Practice

1. We will buy our products at this company in November.[10] It will be better for shopping as prices should be[20] low.

2. I trust that they will try to settle all the labour[10] problems this term. The girls tried to buy better dresses last[20] November, but the labour troubles stopped them.[29]

3. Are you going to address the employees of this[10] company next October? Yes, I will address The Product[20] Sales Force. My address is to be on the rising costs of[30] products today. This is certain to be a growing problem[40] which all manufacturers must face.[47]

4. I hope that the labour forces and the manufacturers[10] try to settle the problems today. They must settle[20] them or we will be unable to stop rising prices and[30] taxes. We regret that your company's problems were not[40] settled last November.

5. The Trader's Store is having an October sale of[10] low-priced paper products. I expect that they will present[20] the prices of a number of the products in today's[30] paper.

6. Dear Sir:

   For some time we have tried to get space in the large[10] shopping plaza that is on the Branch Road, but without success.[20] At present, we are going to locate our company[30] on Water Road. We are glad to let you know that we shall[40] have a larger space in which to prepare better products.[50]

   We hope you will take time to come and celebrate our success[60] at our larger branch store on November 17.

   Yours,[70]

15

Writing the sounds of Ē and Ĭ; third position horizontal strokes; diphones

TOP ①

Unit 1

MiddLe ②

Principle Discovery

If the word *eat* is written ⸺⎸⸺
If the word *lead* is written ⸺⌐⸺ *EnD ③*
If the word *need* is written ⸺◡⸺

can you discover the shorthand signs and principles used in writing the outlines for the words listed below?

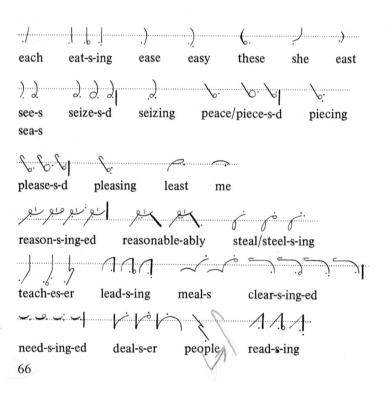

each   eat-s-ing   ease   easy   these   she   east

see-s   seize-s-d   seizing   peace/piece-s-d   piecing
sea-s

please-s-d   pleasing   least   me

reason-s-ing-ed   reasonable-ably   steal/steel-s-ing

teach-es-er   lead-s-ing   meal-s   clear-s-ing-ed

need-s-ing-ed   deal-s-er   people   read-s-ing

66

Pitman Principles

1. The sign for Ē is a dot written near the end of a stroke as in: *eat* ___|___ and *steel* ___/___ .

2. If the first vowel sound in a word is Ē, the first up or down stroke is written through the line as in *please* ___ , *least* ___ , and *east·* ___ . This is known as third position.

3. Write third position words on the line if the outline has no up or down strokes, as in *need* ___ and *me* ___ .

4. When a third position vowel comes between two strokes, write it in front of the second stroke as in *lead* ___ and *meal* ___ .

SKILL-BUILDING PLAN 1

Reading and Writing Practice

1. Read the shorthand outlines in this Unit, preferably repeating the words out loud.

2. Cover the printed words and read the shorthand outlines.

3. Write the shorthand outlines in your notebook until you can write them easily and quickly.

4. Write the shorthand outlines from dictation. Keep your text open as you write. Refer to your text whenever necessary.

5. Read the shorthand which you have taken from dictation.
    YOUR AIM: TO WRITE 50 WORDS A MINUTE

Unit 2

Home work
Page 26

Principle Discovery

If the word *sit* is written ___
If the word *with* is written ___
If the word *simple* is written ___
If the word *since* is written ___

can you discover the shorthand signs and principles used in writing the outlines for the words listed below?

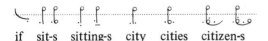

if   sit-s   sitting-s   city   cities   citizen-s

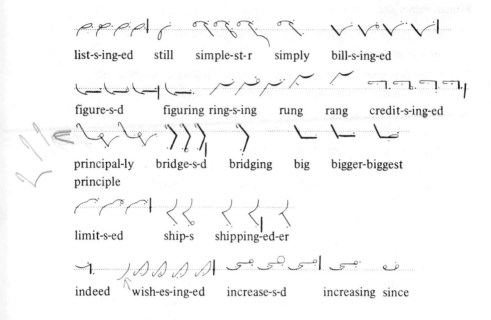

list-s-ing-ed   still   simple-st-r   simply   bill-s-ing-ed

figure-s-d   figuring ring-s-ing   rung   rang   credit-s-ing-ed

principal-ly   bridge-s-d   bridging   big   bigger-biggest
principle

limit-s-ed   ship-s   shipping-ed-er

indeed   wish-es-ing-ed   increase-s-d   increasing since

Pitman Principles

1. The sign for ĭ is a dot written near the end of a stroke, as in *if* ⟍ , *ill* ⌒ and *bill* ⟍ .

2. If the first vowel sound in a word is ĭ, the first up or down stroke is written through the line, as in *with* ⟋ and *bring* ⟍ .

3. Write third position words on the line if the outline has no up or down strokes as in *since* ⟋ and *increase* ⟋ .

Master Unit 2 by following Skill-Building Plan 1 on page 67.

Unit 3

Reading and Writing Practice

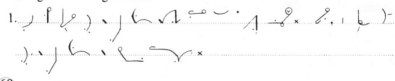

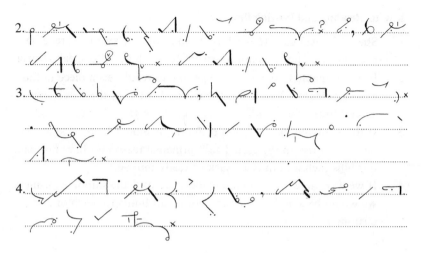

See page 70 for the key to this Unit.

See page 70 for the key to this Unit.

SKILL-BUILDING PLAN 2

Building Reading and Writing Skills

1. Read each sentence until you can read it fluently.
2. Read all the sentences as a unit. Are you reading them without hesitation?
3. Practise writing each sentence in shorthand until you can write it easily and rapidly.
4. Write all the sentences once as a unit.

Building Dictation Skills

1. Practise writing each sentence from dictation. Keep your text open for easy reference.
2. Read the shorthand you have written in your notebook.
3. When you have completed the sentences, follow the same plan to practise a paragraph or a letter.

   YOUR AIM: TO WRITE 60 WORDS A MINUTE

Key to Reading and Writing Practice

1. She said it was easy to teach them to lead the class in[10] a reading exercise. Yes, but it is not so easy[20] to teach them to speak clearly.

2. Is it reasonable to expect these people to read[10] each piece in the exercise clearly? Yes, this is the reason[20] we read these exercises several times. We need[30] to read each piece several times.

3. If this company pays its bills regularly, it should[10] be listed as the best credit risk in the east. The[20] principal reason we have not paid our bills each month is a[30] lack of ready money.

4. If we were able to get a reasonable share of[10] the shipping business, we would be able to increase[20] our credit limits for each of our customers.

Unit 4

Pitman Pacers

think

Phrases

I think   we think   each month   in this city   it is certain

Master Unit 4 by following Skill-Building Plan 1 on page 67.

Unit 5

Building Vocabulary Skills

Note: Two vowels sounded together are called a *diphone*.
Indicate a diphone by the sign . Write the diphone sign in the same place as the first vowel sound in the diphone.

piano-s   idea-s   ideal-ly   radio-s   create-s-d   creating   cooperate-s-d

70

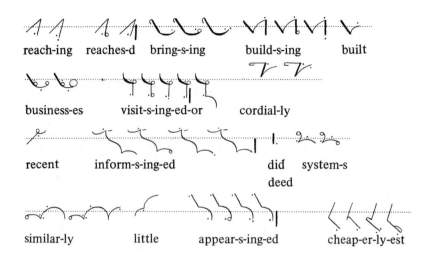

reach-ing   reaches-d   bring-s-ing   build-s-ing   built

business-es   visit-s-ing-ed-or   cordial-ly

recent   inform-s-ing-ed   did   system-s
                                deed

similar-ly   little   appear-s-ing-ed   cheap-er-ly-est

Master Unit 5 by following **Skill-Building Plan 1** on **page 67.**

PUNCTUATION TIP: A hyphen is represented by ......

UNIT 6

Reading and Writing Practice

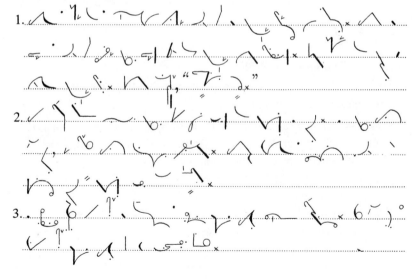

71

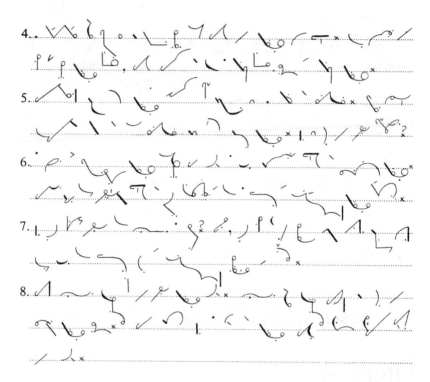

See below for the key to these sentences.

Unit 7

Developing Transcription Skills

To study this Unit, follow Transcription Skill-Building Plan on page 43.

Key to Reading and Writing Practice

1. We have an idea for a monthly radio show[10] on which two piano players will appear. We hope to[20] create a show on which serious pieces created[30] just for the piano will be presented. It should be[40] ideal for people who love piano playing. It[50] will be entitled, "Cordially Yours."[57]

2. We brought back many pieces which are still needed for[10] building the ship. The pieces were not cheap, but the prices were[20] fairly reasonable. We hope that they will have a[30] similar showing of dealer's ship-building needs in October.[40]

3. The citizens of this city are trying to form a[10] system to deal with smoke problems. This is not easy as[20] they are trying to deal with it without increasing taxes.[30]

4. The purpose of this trip is to pick cities in which we[10] think our businesses will grow. If limits are set on the[20] city business taxes, we think we will all have a better[30] tax system and better businesses.[37]

5. We are pleased to have your business and we will try to[10] bring you the best of service. Please let us know if we are[20] able to be of any service to you or to your[30] business. Did you see our recent price list?[37]

6. A list of the principal businesses in this city[10] would show a need to limit the growth of similar[20] businesses. We need to wait for the reasonable growth[30] of shipping facilities and for a clear and informed[40] business policy.

7. Did she tell you the reason for making a speech? Yes, she[10] said that each citizen should be ready to take the lead[20] if the need for clear thinking and informed citizens should[30] arise.

8. We had many visitors at our recent business show.[10] Many of these visitors wished to see our simple business[20] system. We also did a lot of business with them as[30] they were watching our show.[35]

16 Writing the sound of H

UNIT 1

Principle Discovery

If the word *hope* is written
If the word *hotel* is written
If the word *habit* is written
If the word *perhaps* is written

can you discover the shorthand signs and principles used in writing the outlines for the words listed below?

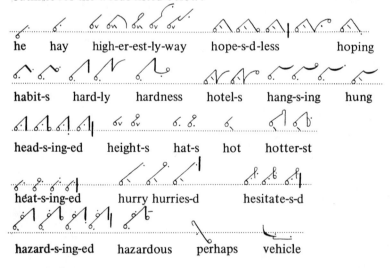

he   hay   high-er-est-ly-way   hope-s-d-less   hoping

habit-s   hard-ly   hardness   hotel-s   hang-s-ing   hung

head-s-ing-ed   height-s   hat-s   hot   hotter-st

heat-s-ing-ed   hurry hurries-d   hesitate-s-d

hazard-s-ing-ed   hazardous   perhaps   vehicle

Pitman Principles

1. The sound of H is generally written _____ as in *hope* _____ .
2. If H is lightly sounded, as in *perhaps*, it is omitted.

Master the outlines in Unit 1 by following Skill-Building Plan 1 on page 67.

74

UNIT 2

Pitman Principles

The sound of H is expressed by a tick in words beginning with M, L, and downward R as in:

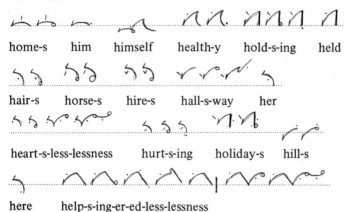

| home-s | him | himself | health-y | hold-s-ing | held |

| hair-s | horse-s | hire-s | hall-s-way | her |

| heart-s-less-lessness | hurt-s-ing | holiday-s | hill-s |

| here | help-s-ing-er-ed-less-lessness |

Master Unit 2 by following Skill-Building Plan 1 on page 67.

UNIT 3

Reading and Writing Practice

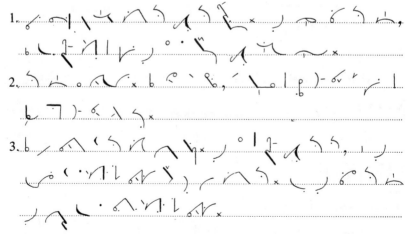

See page 76 for the key to these sentences.
Master Unit 3 by following Skill-Building Plan 2 on page 69.

Key to Reading and Writing Practice

1.   He seemed to be unable to help her with her problem.[10] She must sell her home, but is having trouble holding it[20] till she has a buyer with enough money.[28]
2.   Her home is lovely. It has lots of space, and because it[10] sits so high on the hill it does not get so hot up here.[20]
3.   It is our hope that her health will be better. She has had[10] trouble with her heart, but she feels that a holiday at[20] the hotel by the sea will help her. If she sells her home[30] she will be able to have a happy holiday at[40] the hotel.

UNIT 4

Phrases

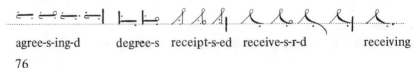

he is   he will   he will be   if you   if you will

if you are   if we   if we will   if we are

Note: When convenient, intersect the stroke D ⌐ for the word *department* as in:

your department   our department   sales department   credit department

Master Unit 4 by following Skill-Building Plan 1 on page 67.

UNIT 5

Building Vocabulary Skills

agree-s-ing-d   degree-s   receipt-s-ed   receive-s-r-d   receiving

76

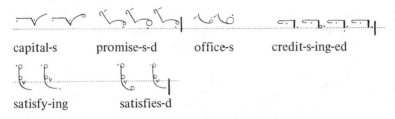

capital-s   promise-s-d   office-s   credit-s-ing-ed

satisfy-ing   satisfies-d

Master Unit 5 by following Skill-Building Plan 1 on page 67.

Unit 6

Reading and Writing Practice

4.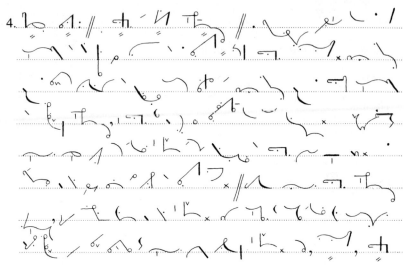

See below for the key to this Unit.

Master Unit 6 by following Skill-Building Plan 2 on page 69.

Unit 7

Developing Transcription Skills

Follow the Transcription Skill-Building Plan 1 on page 43.

Key to Reading and Writing Practice

1. If we see a home with a high hallway which is also[10] located in the hills, we will not hesitate to buy[20] it for him. Of course, the price must not be too high or[30] he will not be able to raise the money this year.[40]

2. We hope to stay at the High Hills Hotel on our visit[10] with you this month. We hope that we shall be able to miss[20] some of the highway hazards on this trip. Perhaps we should[30] buy a larger car. Perhaps we should have a better[40] vehicle for a long holiday trip. Please let me know[50] if you think this idea is all right.[57]

3. Please let our sales department know in a couple of days[10] the number of people who will come to the hotel with[20] you. I will try to hold enough space for all of them. We[30] shall sell any space we have left in the hotel.[39]

78

4.   Dear Mr. Head:

Credit Department and Charge Customers[10]

The principal reason for a large number of bad[20] debts is the lack of a hard-hearted credit manager.[30] You may appear to have a higher level of business[40] in your sales department and you may appear to have a[50] greater number of satisfied customers, but credit[60] that is too easy is hazardous for any firm. I[70] think you will agree that the money must reach your office[80] on time or the benefits of credit will not go to[90] you. A promise to pay is not the same as the receipt[100] of hard cash.

We have many credit customers each month,[110] but we expect them to pay on time. You will notice that[120] in this office they nearly always satisfy our high[130] hopes that the money will be received on time.

Yours,[140]

Manager, Credit Department

17

Writing the sounds of OO, OO, and U

UNIT 1

Principle Discovery

If the word *blue* is written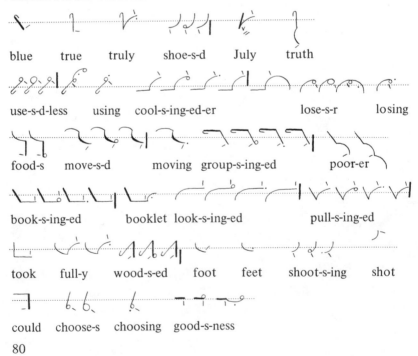

If the word *cool* is written

If the word *foot* is written

If the word *took* is written

can you discover the shorthand signs and principles used in writing the outlines for the words listed below?

blue true truly shoe-s-d July truth

use-s-d-less using cool-s-ing-ed-er lose-s-r losing

food-s move-s-d moving group-s-ing-ed poor-er

book-s-ing-ed booklet look-s-ing-ed pull-s-ing-ed

took full-y wood-s-ed foot feet shoot-s-ing shot

could choose-s choosing good-s-ness

80

Pitman Principles

1. The sound $\overline{OO}$ and all related OO sounds are represented by a dash written at the end of a stroke in third position as in *blue* ⟍, *cool* ⟋ and *took* ⌐.

2. The first up or down stroke is written through the line if $\overline{OO}$ or any related OO sound, is the first vowel sound in a word as in *lose* ⟋, *choose* ↓, *move* ⟍, and *foot* ⌣.

Master Unit 1 by following Skill-Building Plan 1 on page 67.

UNIT 2

Principle Discovery

If the word *beauty* is written ⟍

If the word *duty* is written |

If the word *issue* is written ⟋

If the word *valuable* is written ⟍⟍

can you discover the shorthand signs and principles used in writing the outlines for the words listed below?

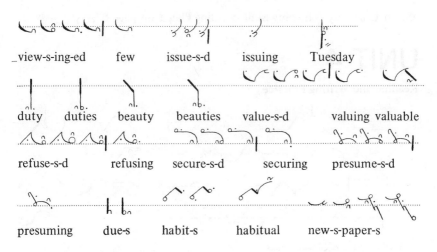

_view-s-ing-ed	few	issue-s-d	issuing	Tuesday
duty	duties	beauty	beauties	value-s-d	valuing valuable
refuse-s-d	refusing	secure-s-d	securing	presume-s-d
presuming	due-s	habit-s	habitual	new-s-paper-s

81

Pitman Principles

1. The sound Ū is represented by the sign ....ɔ.... written in third position, as in *duty* ⌐ᵢ, *beauty* ↘ᵢᵢ, and *due* ⌐ₕ·

2. The first up or down stroke is written through the line if the first sound in a word is Ū as in *newspaper* ↘⸜ and *Tuesday* |ₓ·

3. The sign for Ū is sometimes joined to a stroke, as in *few* ⌣ₙ, *new* ⌣ₗ, *issue* ⌐ₗ, and *value* ⌣ᶜ.

4. A small tick added to the sign for Ū indicates a following vowel sound as in *valuable* ⌣⸜ and *habitual* ⌐⌣.

Master Unit 2 by following Skill-Building Plan 1 on page 67.

UNIT 3

Phrases

Note: A shaded tick may be used for *he* in the middle or at the end of a phrase.

if he   if he is   if he will   if he will be   Yours truly

Master Unit 3 by following Skill-Building Plan 1 on page 67.

UNIT 4

Reading and Writing Practice

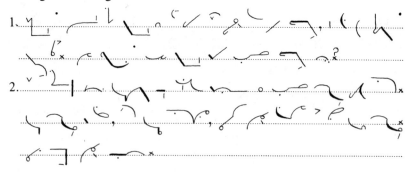

82

See below for the key to this Unit.

Master Unit 4 by following Skill-Building Plan 2 on page 69.

UNIT 5

Developing Transcription Skills

To develop your Transcribing Skills follow the Transcription Skill-Building Plan on page 43.

Key to Reading and Writing Practice

1.   I took a look at the book you thought we might use for our[10] group, but they think it would be a poor choice. Will you bring a[20] new book to our next group meeting?[26]

2. I asked him if he will be good enough to make his[10] next move with care. If he moves too fast, or if he is[20] careless, he will lose the value of the last few moves. He could[30] lose the game.

3. I hope we shall be able to secure some good ideas[10] that deal with subjects of real value to our[20] business. If we look for good ideas this month, we may[30] be able to use them in the July issue of our[40] News Magazine.

4. If you move to your new home in the woods next July, will[10] you be taking any of your valuable books with[20] you or will you leave them at the office?[28]

5. Dear Mr. Parker:

    I presume that the reason you refused[10] to come to our group meeting last Tuesday is also[20] the reason you refuse to come to our next meeting. It[30] is not true that we use our group meetings for the purpose[40] of securing customers. In our view this would not be[50] the right way to act and I assure you that it is not[60] our habit to use our meetings for any reason which[70] would not be acceptable to all who come. I hope you[80] will be able to see your way clear to come to the Book[90] Building on Tuesday, November 10.

    I shall look for you[100] in the large group which we expect to appear at the meeting.[110]

                    Yours truly,

18 Writing the sound of OW; downward L

UNIT 1

Principle Discovery

If the word *out* is written ......|....

If the word *mouth* is written ....⟩...

If the word *power* is written ..\......

can you discover the shorthand signs and principles used in writing the outlines for the words listed below?

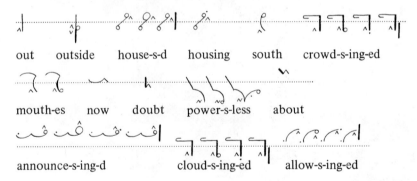

out   outside   house-s-d   housing   south   crowd-s-ing-ed

mouth-es   now   doubt   power-s-less   about

announce-s-ing-d   cloud-s-ing-ed   allow-s-ing-ed

Pitman Principles

1. The sound OW is represented by ....⌃.... written in third position to a stroke as in *out* ...|...
2. The first upstroke or downstroke is written through the line if the first vowel sound in a word is OW as in *house* ..⟩.. and *out* ...|...
3. Strokes with joined OW may be halved for the addition of T or D as in *doubt* ..⊩..

4. A small tick added to OW indicates a following vowel sound as in *power* ⌇.

Master Unit 1 by following Skill-Building Plan 1 on page 67.

UNIT 2

Principle Discovery

If the word *only* is written ⌇.
If the word *recently* is written ⌇.

If the word *certainly* is written ⌇.

If the word *wrongly* is written ⌇.
If the word *increasingly* is written ⌇.

can you discover the shorthand signs and principles used in writing the outlines for the words listed below?

only   unless   annual-ly   certainly   until   evidently

recently   accordingly   increasingly   analyze   analysis

Pitman Principles

1. L is written downward after N and NG.
2. The sound INGLY is usually expressed by NG and downward L as in *kingly* ⌇.

Master Unit 2 by following Skill-Building Plan 1 on page 67.

UNIT 3

Reading and Writing Practice

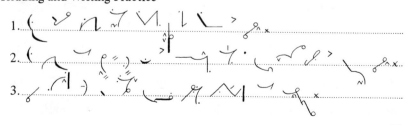

1.
2.
3.

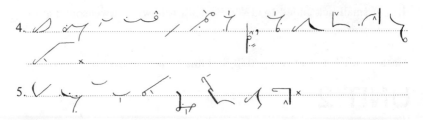

4. ....

5. ....

See below for the key to these sentences.

Master Unit 3 by following Skill-Building Plan 2 on page 69.

Key to Reading and Writing Practice

1. They have always held the annual party outside at[10] the back of the house.
2. They live in the South-East end of the county only a[10] few miles west of the power house.[16]
3. He allowed us to analyze the figures recently[10] reported in the news-papers.[16]
4. We shall certainly not announce our results until[10] Tuesday, unless we have time allowed for this work.
5. They are evidently in no hurry to discuss the[10] problem with the crowd.

Unit 4

Building Vocabulary Skills

Remember: Write third position words on the line if there are no up or downstrokes.

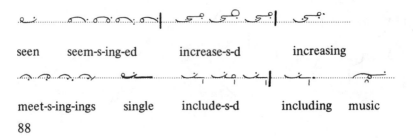

seen   seem-s-ing-ed   increase-s-d   increasing

meet-s-ing-ings   single   include-s-d   including   music

88

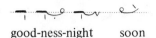

good-ness-night   soon

Remember: The first vowel sound determines the position of the outline.

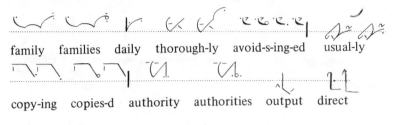

family   families   daily   thorough-ly   avoid-s-ing-ed   usual-ly

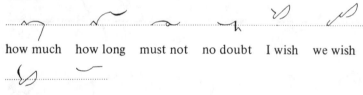

copy-ing   copies-d   authority   authorities   output   direct

Master Unit 4 by following Skill-Building Plan 1 on page 67.

Unit 5

Note: The Pitman Pacer for *how* is ....∧...

Phrases

how much   how long   must not   no doubt   I wish   we wish

they wish   in fact

Master Unit 5 by following Skill-Building Plan 1 on page 67.

Unit 6

Reading and Writing Practice

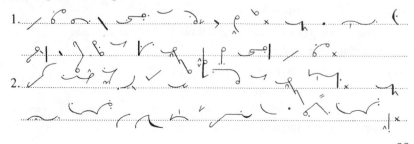

See below for the key to this Unit.

Master Unit 6 by following Skill-Building Plan 2 on page 69.

Unit 7

Developing Transcription Skills

To develop your Transcribing Skill follow the Transcription Skill-Building Plan on page 43.

Key to Reading and Writing Practice

1. Our sales seem to be increasing in areas to the[10] south of us. No doubt the money they used to purchase space[20] in the daily newspapers outside the city increased[30] our sales.

2. We will announce the annual showing of our new cars[10] in the news-
    paper on Monday. No doubt many families[20] will leave home on the
    weekend for a happy family[30] outing. We expect a great crowd at
    the sale; in fact, we[40] are hoping for a full house. We think the prices
    of our[50] cars will allow each customer to save enough money[60] to
    purchase a small car, also.

3. We wish that we could avoid increasing the price of our[10] goods, but
    it seems that rising costs leave us powerless to[20] avoid new increases.
    We must not produce goods of poor[30] value. If we do, we shall miss
    our usual annual[40] increase in customer sales.[45]

4. Dear Miss Maxwell:

    No doubt this is the right time to include[10] the local authorities in
    our group meetings. They should[20] be included now unless it is
    already too late[30] for this year. Unless we have help with our tax
    problems, we[40] will be powerless to make any change in the business[50]
    tax we must pay.

    We need to make a full analysis[60] of the changes which took place
    recently, if we are[70] to have a case for reduced taxes. Accordingly,[80]
    at our next meeting I will move that we start direct face[90]-to-face
    talks with the local tax authorities about[100] our particular problems.

                            Yours truly,[107]

19

Writing the sound of N to curved strokes

UNIT 1

Principle Discovery

If the word *known* is written ⟨shorthand⟩

If the word *amount* is written ⟨shorthand⟩

If the word *payment* is written ⟨shorthand⟩

If the word *machines* is written ⟨shorthand⟩

can you discover the shorthand signs and principles used in writing the outlines for the words listed below?

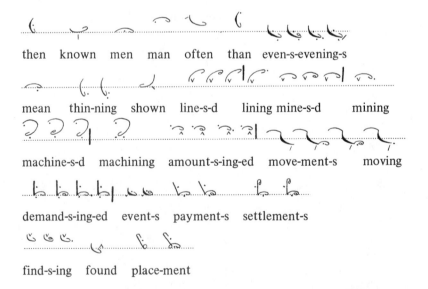

then   known   men   man   often   than   even-s-evening-s

mean   thin-ning   shown   line-s-d   lining mine-s-d   mining

machine-s-d   machining   amount-s-ing-ed   move-ment-s   moving

demand-s-ing-ed   event-s   payment-s   settlement-s

find-s-ing   found   place-ment

Note: fun ⟨shorthand⟩ *but funny* ⟨shorthand⟩ *; men* ⟨shorthand⟩ *but many* ⟨shorthand⟩ *.*

92

Pitman Principles

1. A small hook inside the end of a curve adds N, as in *then* (⟨ and *machine* ⟨⟩.

2. The S-circle is written inside the hook, as in *lines* ⟨⟩ and *mines* ⟨⟩.

3. The hooked stroke may be halved to add the T or D sound as in *amount* ⟨⟩ and *demand* ⟨⟩.

4. The hook N is not used when a vowel ends the word.

Master Unit 1 by following Skill-Building Plan 1 on **page 67.**

Unit 2

Phrases

1. We can add the word *not* to a phrase by halving the stroke and adding the N-hook, as in:

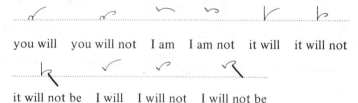

you will   you will not   I am   I am not   it will   it will not

it will not be   I will   I will not   I will not be

2. The N-hook is also used to express the word *been* in a phrase as in:

I have been   we have been   should have been

Master Unit 2 by following Skill-Building Plan 1 on **page 67.**

Unit 3

Building Vocabulary Skills

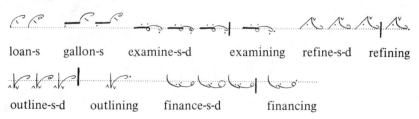

loan-s   gallon-s   examine-s-d   examining   refine-s-d   refining

outline-s-d   outlining   finance-s-d   financing

telephone-s-d telephoning amend-s-ing-ed excellent

enjoyment within necessary refund-s-ing-ed

Master Unit 3 by following Skill-Building Plan 1 on page 67.

Unit 4

Reading and Writing Practice

1.

2.

3.

4.

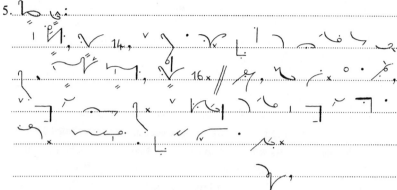

5.

See below for the key to this Unit.

Master Unit 4 by following Skill-Building Plan 2 on page 69.

Unit 5

Developing Transcription Skills

To develop your Transcribing Skill follow the Transcription Skill-Building plan on page 43.

Key to Reading and Writing Practice

1. We have been hoping to be able to purchase a[10] number of the new refining machines within the next few[20] days, but we now fear that they will not be ready in time.[30] A member of the management of the firm which supplies[40] these machines telephoned to say that they have been having[50] trouble with a large number of shipments.

2. You will be pleased to hear that we have just received a[10] new telephone, a new telephone number, and a new[20] telephone line. This must be the result of our demands[30] for better service. Perhaps our statement that we would not[40] make a payment on our telephone bill until they found[50] the trouble on our line had an excellent effect.[60]

3. Now that we have our new building, it will be necessary[10] to find a new and excellent means of financing the[20] loan which we raised to pay for it. We will outline our needs[30] and examine all means of securing the amount of[40] money we need to make a reasonable settlement. We do[50] not expect any unreasonable demands for payment.[60]

4. Will you please mail me a copy of my monthly statement.[10] I am moving out of the city and I would like to[20] make a full settlement of all my loan payments. Since[30] movement of the mail in this part of the city is known to[40] be slow, perhaps you could find time to telephone me, too.[50]

5. Dear Mr. Found:

On Saturday, April 14, I[10] purchased an airline ticket at your main office for the noon[20] trip to Montreal on Monday, April 16.

Recently,[30] I have been ill. As a result, I could not make the trip.[40] I telephoned your office but could not get an answer.[50] I am enclosing the ticket and would like a refund.[60]

Yours truly,

20 Writing the sound of N to straight strokes

Unit 1

Principle Discovery

If the word *run* is written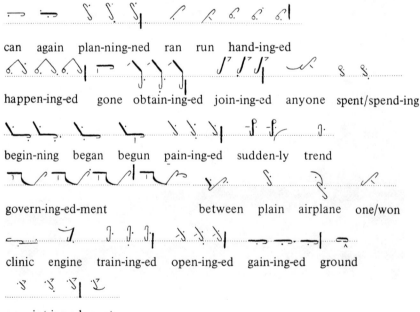
If the word *count* is written
If the word *paint* is written
If the word *appointment* is written

can you discover the shorthand signs and principles used in writing the outlines for the words listed below?

can again plan-ning-ned ran run hand-ing-ed

happen-ing-ed gone obtain-ing-ed join-ing-ed anyone spent/spend-ing

begin-ning began begun pain-ing-ed sudden-ly trend

govern-ing-ed-ment between plain airplane one/won

clinic engine train-ing-ed open-ing-ed gain-ing-ed ground

appoint-ing-ed-ment

98

Pitman Principles

1. A small hook at the end of a straight stroke written on the non-circle side adds the sound of N as in *again* ...., *plan* , *obtain* , and *sudden* .

2. The hooked stroke may be halved to add T or D as in *trend* ..

3. In some cases ENT is used for MENT to make an easier joining as in *appointment* and *announcement* .

4. The sound LY is sometimes shown by disjoined L as in *suddenly* .

Master Unit 1 by following Skill-Building Plan 1 on page 67.

Unit 2

Note: The Pitman Pacer for *cannot* is ....

Phrases

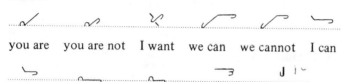

you are   you are not   I want   we can   we cannot   I can

I cannot   you can   you cannot   can you   had not

Master Unit 2 by following Skill-Building Plan 1 on page 67.

Unit 3

Reading and Writing Practice

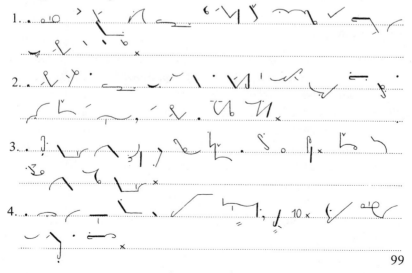

5.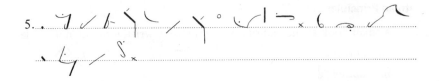

SKILL BUILDING PLAN 2

Building Reading and Writing Skills

1. Read each sentence until you can read it fluently.
2. Read all the sentences as a unit. Are you reading them without hesitation?
3. Practise writing each sentence in shorthand until you can write it easily and rapidly.
4. Write all the sentences once as a unit.

Building Dictation Skills

1. Practise writing each sentence from dictation. Keep your text open for easy reference.
2. Read the shorthand you have written in your notebook.
3. When you have completed the sentences, follow the same plan to practise a paragraph or a letter.

YOUR AIM: TO WRITE 70 WORDS A MINUTE.

Key to Reading and Writing Practice

1. The success of the public health clinic that is operated[10] by the members of our group will need the support of[20] all of us.
2. The support of such a clinic need not be a burden[10] on anyone if we agree to spend a little time and[20] money, and support the authorities in charge.[29]
3. The training booklet will be issued to each person at[10] the time the plan is settled. Times of your appointments will[20] be in this booklet.
4. The men will go back to work on Monday, June 10. They were[10] successful in obtaining an agreement.[18]
5. The engine we just bought for our boat has failed again.[10] This means we will have to change our plan.[17]

100

Unit 4

Building Vocabulary Skills

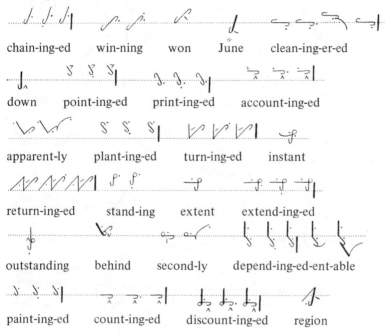

chain-ing-ed   win-ning   won   June   clean-ing-er-ed

down   point-ing-ed   print-ing-ed   account-ing-ed

apparent-ly   plant-ing-ed   turn-ing-ed   instant

return-ing-ed   stand-ing   extent   extend-ing-ed

outstanding   behind   second-ly   depend-ing-ed-ent-able

paint-ing-ed   count-ing-ed   discount-ing-ed   region

Master Unit 4 by following Skill-Building Plan 1 on page 67.

Unit 5

Reading and Writing Practice

1.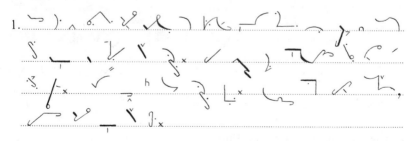

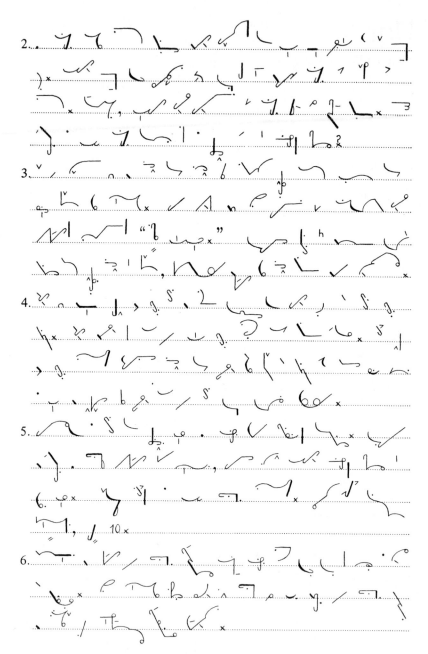

See page 103 for the key to this Unit.

Master Unit 5 by following Skill-Building Plan 2 on page 100.

Unit 6

Developing Transcription Skills

TRANSCRIPTION SKILL-BUILDING PLAN

For the last few lessons we have been following two steps in the development of transcribing skills. In this plan we suggest that you drop Step 1 and begin your transcription directly from your own shorthand notes. If you find that transcribing directly from your own notes causes you difficulty, continue the two-step plan for several more lessons. The point at which Step 1 should be dropped is always a matter of individual judgment.

1. Write the sentences from the preceding unit in shorthand from dictation. Then
   (*a*) Read your shorthand notes. Insert the punctuation. If you are not sure of the spelling of a word, check it in your dictionary before you begin to transcribe.
   (*b*) Transcribe these sentences from your own notes.
2. Follow the above plan when transcribing a letter.

Key to Reading and Writing Practice

1. I cannot say how happy I was to receive your[10] telephone call asking me to join you in your plan to go[20] to Ottawa by airplane. We should be able to see[30] the government passing laws and appointing judges. I[40] will count on you for the airplane ticket. If you cannot[50] get one in time, we can always go by train.[58]

2. The engine in this car began to run wild for no good[10] reason that I could see. Anyone could have been seriously[20] hurt if he had been caught between the engine and the[30] side of the car. Fortunately, no one was working on[40] the engine just as the trouble began. Can you obtain[50] a new engine for me at a discount and on extended terms?[60]

3. I should like you to account for the amount which is[10] apparently outstanding in your name for the second[20] time this month. We wrote to you last week but the envelope[30] was returned marked "Address unknown." If we cannot[40] depend on you to make full payment of your outstanding[50] account on time, it will be necessary to turn this account[60] back to our lawyers.

4.   I want you to go down to the printing plant to ask if[10] you can have one sheet of plain printing paper. I want to[20] use it in our own printing machine in the back office.[30] Point out to the printing manager that we can account[40] for the use of this type of paper and that I can send[50] him a note to outline its use in our plant if he feels[60] this is necessary.

5.   We must have a plan for discounting notes the instant they[10] are presented for payment. If we are to obtain the[20] greatest return on our money, we cannot allow[30] anyone extended terms on these notes. I have just appointed[40] a new credit manager. He will join the firm on Monday,[50] June 10.

6.   I am going to turn our credit problems into[10] instant cash even if it means a loss of business. Last month's[20] statement shows how great is the need to train our credit[30] people to analyse each customer's prospects thoroughly.[40]

21

Writing the sounds NS, NZ, NSES, NST, and NSTER at the end of straight strokes

Unit 1

Principle Discovery

If the word *dance* is written ....

If the word *points* is written ....

If the word *chances* is written ....

If the word *against* is written ....

If the word *spinster* is written ....

can you discover the shorthand signs and principles used in writing the outlines for the words listed below?

dance-s-d   dancing   chance-s-d   chancing   point-s-ing-ed   bond-s

distance-s   distancing   expense-s   expensive   response-s   responsive

account-s   turn-s   learn-s-ing-ed   rent-s-ing-ed

assist-s-ing-ed-ance-ant   instance-s   train-s-ing-ed

kind-s-ly-ness-est   spin-s-ing-ster-s   clean-s-ing-ed

maintain-s-ing-ed

106

Pitman Principles

1. We add S to a straight stroke hooked for N by closing the circle to represent the sound NS as in *dance* and *cleanse* .

2. We add SES to a straight stroke hooked for N to represent the sound NSES as in *dances* and *cleanses* .

3. We add ST to a straight stroke hooked for N to represent the sound NST as in *against* .

4. We add STER to a straight stroke hooked for N to represent the sound NSTER as in *spinster* .

Master Unit 1 by following Skill-Building Plan 1 on page 67.

Unit 2

Pitman Pacers

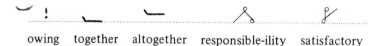

owing   together   altogether   responsible-ility   satisfactory

Phrases

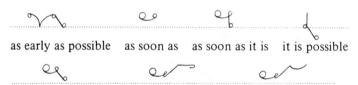

as early as possible   as soon as   as soon as it is   it is possible

as soon as possible   as soon as we can   as soon as we know

Master Unit 2 by following Skill-Building Plan 1 on page 67.

Unit 3

Reading and Writing Practice

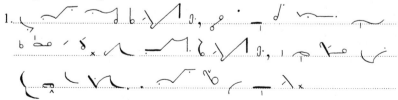

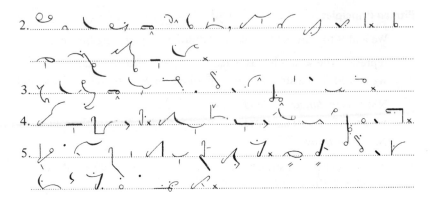

See below for the key to these sentences.

Master Unit 3 by following Skill-Building Plan 2 on page 100.

Key to Reading and Writing Practice

1. If the market maintains its upward trend, he has a good[10] chance of making money on his stocks and bonds. We have no[20] guarantee of this upward trend, but most brokers feel they have[30] grounds for believing the market prices will go up.[40]
2. As soon as you have seen the grounds around this home, we know[10] you will wish to rent it. It is most impressive and we[20] think it is good value.
3. I think you have sufficient grounds for not accepting the[10] plans to allow discounts on all new accounts.[18]
4. We will go directly to the train. We have no time to[10] go to the office now as the distance is too great.[20]
5. It was a long trip but we had no trouble with the engine.[10] Mr. Jones plans to tell them that the engine is an excellent[20] one.

Unit 4

Building Vocabulary Skills

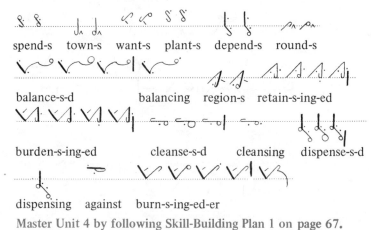

spend-s   town-s   want-s   plant-s   depend-s   round-s

balance-s-d   balancing   region-s   retain-s-ing-ed

burden-s-ing-ed   cleanse-s-d   cleansing   dispense-s-d

dispensing   against   burn-s-ing-ed-er

Master Unit 4 by following Skill-Building Plan 1 on **page 67.**

Unit 5

Reading and Writing Practice

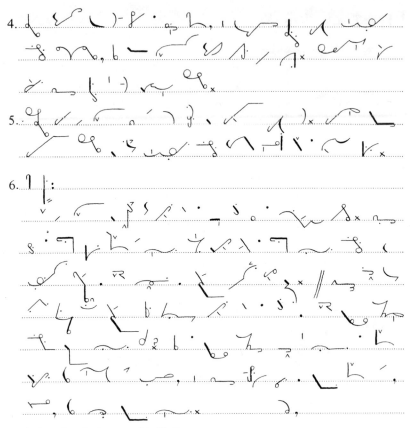

See below for the key to this Unit.

Master Unit 5 by following Skill-Building Plan 2 on page 100.

Unit 6

Developing Transcription Skills

To develop your Transcribing Skill follow the Transcription Skill-Building Plan on page 103.

Key to Reading and Writing Practice

1. No one should obtain a line of credit without opening[10] the books of his firm for a close analysis of[20] his outstanding accounts. I hope you agree with this[30] idea since I will be looking to you for assistance[40] if this plan runs into trouble. I intend to begin[50] this plan within one week.

110

2. In this instance it is most satisfactory to learn[10] that the chances for success are now so much better. You[20] can depend on us to maintain the kinds of high class stores[30] you will be glad to be responsible for. In these stores we[40] can dispense the finest products sold in any of the[50] towns for a distance of at least 25 miles around.[60]

3. We can retain our present high level of business for[10] the balance of the year. How we do for the rest of the[20] year depends upon how responsive our business becomes[30] to the burdens and chances involved in running a[40] chain of stores as large as this one. [46]

4. It is possible that we will not have so satisfactory[10] a second term, but if we can dispense with unnecessary[20] expenses as early as possible, it is[30] altogether likely that we shall retain our lead.[40] As soon as we know the whole story you can depend on[50] us to let you know as soon as possible.[58]

5. As soon as it is possible we should like you and your[10] assistant to work with us. We must begin work as soon[20] as possible to avoid the unnecessary[30] expense that will be caused by a long delay.[38]

6. Dear Ted:

    I should like to point out that the running of a[10] good band is an important responsibility. You[20] can spend a great deal of time and money only to run[30] up a great many expenses without necessarily[40] producing the kind of music the public really wants[50] to hear.

    How can you account for the rapid changes in[60] public taste which make the running of a band the kind of[70] business in which you must expect to take many chances?[80] It is a business in which you cannot count on making[90] a dime between this month and the next, but you can suddenly[100] hit the big time and, of course, this means big money.

    Yours,[110]

22

Writing the sounds of
FR, VR, THR, SHR,
MR, NR; FL, VL, NL,
ML, THL, SHL

Unit 1

Principle Discovery

If the word *ever* is written

If the word *either* is written

If the word *dinner* is written

If the word *measure* is written

If the word *summer* is written

If the word *sooner* is written

If the word *safer* is written

can you discover the shorthand signs and principles used in writing the outlines for the words listed below?

ever   everyone   offer-s-ing-ed   either   either   author   other-wise

honour-s-ing-ed   Friday   average-s-d   averaging   differ-s-ing-ed-ence-ent

dinner-s   perform-s-ing-ed-ance   manner-s   measure-s-d

measuring   enclosure   favour-s-ing-ed-able   summer-s   safer

sooner   from   over   pressure

112

Pitman Principles

1. A small hook at the beginning of the curved stroke adds the sound of R to form the double consonant sounds FR, VR, etc.

2. A small circle written inside the hook adds the sound of S as in *safer* ⌒.

Master Unit 1 by following Skill-Building Plan 1 on page 67.

Unit 2

Principal Discovery

If the word *flow* is written ⌒

If the word *travel* is written ⌒

If the word *powerful* is written ⌏

If the word *personal* is written ⌒

can you discover the shorthand signs and principles used in writing the outlines for the words listed below?

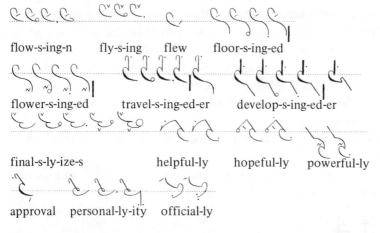

flow-s-ing-n   fly-s-ing   flew   floor-s-ing-ed

flower-s-ing-ed   travel-s-ing-ed-er   develop-s-ing-ed-er

final-s-ly-ize-s   helpful-ly   hopeful-ly   powerful-ly

approval   personal-ly-ity   official-ly

Pitman Principle

1. A large hook at the beginning of a curved stroke adds the sound of L to form the double consonant sounds of FL, VL, etc.

2. Where the hooked form joins easily, it forms the suffix FULL or FULLY.

Master Unit 2 by following Skill-Building Plan 1 on page 67.

Unit 3

Reading and Writing Practice

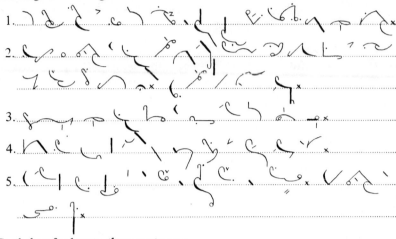

See below for key to these sentences.

Master Unit 3 by following Skill-Building Plan 2 on page 100.

Key to Reading and Writing Practice

1. Your personal approval of the efforts of your[10] employees to develop different sporting facilities[20] would be most helpful.

2. Everyone is hopeful that favourable results will be[10] obtained from the measures we have taken and the manner[20] in which the final plans were made. These results are long overdue.[30]

3. Please let me know the most favourable terms that you can[10] offer on your summer goods. [15]

4. It will be safer if you do not put too much pressure[10] on the floor over the hall. [15]

5. They offered free dinners on all flights to travellers flying[10] to France. They are hopeful of increasing trade.[20]

Unit 4

Principle Discovery

If the word *cover* is written

If the word *gather* is written

If the word *novel* is written

If the word *reflect* is written

114

can you discover the shorthand signs and principles used in writing the outlines for the words listed below?

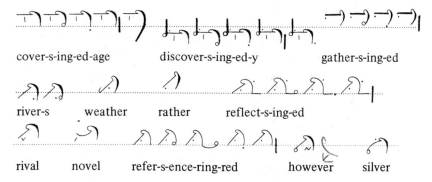

cover-s-ing-ed-age   discover-s-ing-ed-y   gather-s-ing-ed

river-s   weather   rather   reflect-s-ing-ed

rival   novel   refer-s-ence-ring-red   however   silver

Pitman Principles

1. The reversed forms of FR, VR, THR, Thr, FL, and VL are used after horizontal and upstrokes as in *gather* 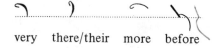, *river* ⌒, and *novel* ⌒. They are used to give an easier joining.

Master Unit 4 by following Skill-Building Plan 1 on page 67.

UNIT 5

Pitman Pacers

very   there/their   more   before

Phrases

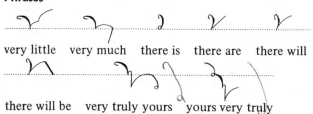

very little   very much   there is   there are   there will

there will be   very truly yours   yours very truly

Master Unit 5 by following Skill-Building Plan 1 on page 67.

Unit 6

Reading and Writing Practice

1.

2.

3.

4.

See page 117 for the key to this Unit.

Master Unit 6 by following Skill-Building Plan 2 on page 100.

Unit 7

Developing Transcription Skills

To develop your Transcribing Skill follow the Transcription Skill-Building Plan on page 103.

Key to Reading and Writing Practice

1. It will be some time before they will be able to discover[10] the cause of the trouble. The airplane was flying in[20] favourable weather. Its powerful engines were apparently[30] working in a satisfactory manner. The knowledge[40] already gathered by officials does not reflect any[50] particular reason for the problem.[58]

2. The people regularly travelling by air will now[10] go either by train or by boat. A great deal more pressure[20] will be placed on the authorities to try to develop[30] safer flights. Your personal approval of the manner[40] in which the airline employees have acted would be a[50] most helpful measure.

3. It could mean the difference between happy employees[10] feeling that their work is looked at favourably or it[20] could result in very bad feelings within the firm. If[30] you could make an offer to them at the dinner next Friday,[40] it would have a very favourable effect on the[50] manner in which their work will be performed.[58]

4. Dear Miss Flowers:

   I am sorry to find that it is necessary[10] to take the measures outlined in the offer enclosed with[20] this memorandum. The enclosure outlines the measures we[30] will take and the manner in which we will take these measures.[40] Our average costs this summer have been rising so fast[50] that they have finally forced us to refer our performance[60] figures to the accounts office for analysis. However,[70] from this day until we have gathered the results of our[80] analysis, we will be very careful not to let[90] our costs go over the average performance figures for[100] the last month.

   In the meantime, there is very little we[110] can do which will reflect favourably on our performance[120] until we can carry out the measures I have suggested.[130]

                    Yours very truly,

Enc.

23 Writing the sounds of F and V to straight strokes

UNIT 1

Principle Discovery

If the word *above* is written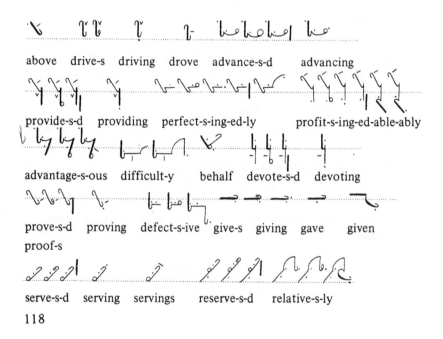

If the word *reserves* is written

If the word *half* is written

If the word *profit* is written

can you discover the shorthand signs and principles used in writing the outlines for the words listed below?

above   drive-s   driving   drove   advance-s-d   advancing

provide-s-d   providing   perfect-s-ing-ed-ly   profit-s-ing-ed-able-ably

advantage-s-ous   difficult-y   behalf   devote-s-d   devoting

prove-s-d   proving   defect-s-ive   give-s   giving   gave   given
proof-s

serve-s-d   serving   servings   reserve-s-d   relative-s-ly

118

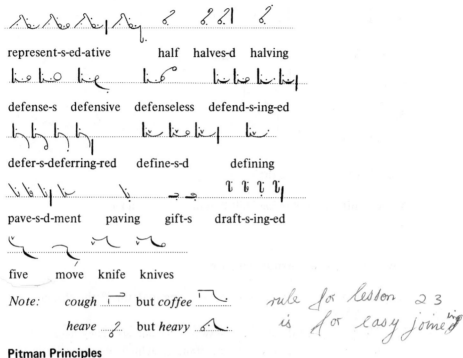

represent-s-ed-ative   half   halves-d   halving

defense-s   defensive   defenseless   defend-s-ing-ed

defer-s-deferring-red   define-s-d   defining

pave-s-d-ment   paving   gift-s   draft-s-ing-ed

five   move   knife   knives

Note: cough ⌐ but *coffee* ⌐⌐   *rule for lesson 23*

heave ↗ but *heavy* ⌐   *is for easy joiner*

Pitman Principles

1. A small hook at the end of a *straight stroke only* adds the sound of F or V as in *above* \ and *half* ⸗.
2. It is written on the same side as circle S.
3. A final S circle is written inside the hook as in *serves* ⸗.
4. A hooked stroke may be halved for T and D as in *drafts* ⸗.
5. The stroke F or V is used when a vowel ends the word as in *coffee* ⌐.
6. There is no F or V hook to curved strokes as in *five* ⸗.

Master Unit 1 by following Skill-Building Plan 1 on page 67.

UNIT 2

Reading and Writing Practice

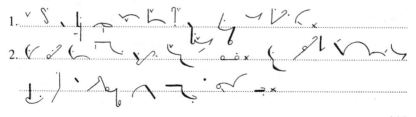

1.

2.

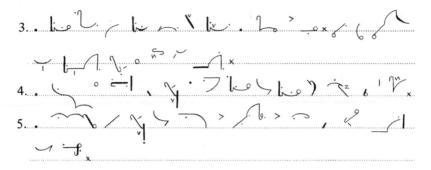

3.

4.

5.

See below for the key to these sentences.

Master Unit 2 by following Skill-Building Plan 2 on page 100.

Key to Reading and Writing Practice

1. I plan to devote most of my time trying to define[10] the changes in the tariff law.[15]
2. They will serve them coffee between five and six. They have reserved[10] the ballroom for the dinner at which all representatives[20] will be given a small gift.[25]
3. The defence attorney will defend him by defining[10] the terms of the case. He thinks he will have no difficulty[20] proving his client not guilty.[26]
4. The firm has agreed to provide a cash advance for the[10] defence of their employee who is on trial.[19]
5. The members are providing for the care of the relatives[10] of the man who was killed in the accident.[19]

UNIT 3

Phrases

1. The F/V hook is used to express *of* in phrases as in:

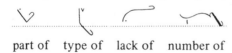

part of   type of   lack of   number of

120

2. The F/V hook is used to express *have* in phrases as in:

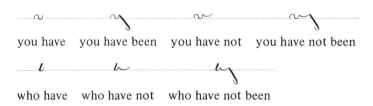

you have   you have been   you have not   you have not been

who have   who have not   who have not been

Master Unit 3 by following Skill-Building Plan 1 on page 67.

UNIT 4

Building Vocabulary Skills

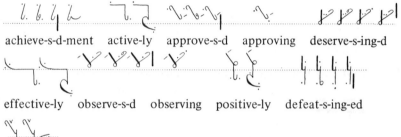

achieve-s-d-ment   active-ly   approve-s-d   approving   deserve-s-ing-d

effective-ly   observe-s-d   observing   positive-ly   defeat-s-ing-ed

private-ly

Master the outlines in Unit 4 by following Skill-Building Plan 1
on page 67.

UNIT 5

Reading and Writing Practice

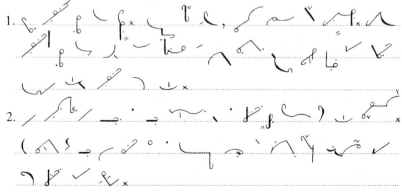

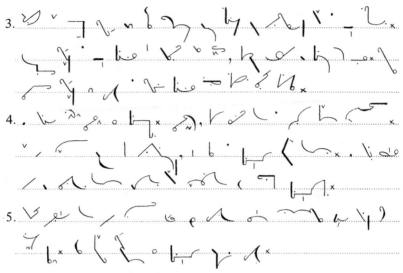

3.

4.

5.

See below for the key to this Unit.

Master Unit 5 by following Skill-Building plan 2 on page 100.

UNIT 6

Developing Transcription Skills

To develop your Transcribing Skill follow the Transcription Skill-Building Plan on page 103.

Key to Reading and Writing Practice

1. Please reserve the seats for Thursday. If he cannot drive over,[10] he will let us know by Wednesday. We have reserved seats for[20] the show in advance and will be happy to have you use[30] the tickets on our behalf if you are unable to reserve[40] your own.

2. Our relatives are giving a gift of money to a[10] deserving student from their own high school. They hope that the[20] gift will serve as an effective means of helping private[30] individuals who are very deserving of our[40] support.

3. I wish I could prove to you that it is very much to[10] your advantage to be represented by a good[20] attorney. If he can provide a good defence on behalf[30] of his client, it will not be necessary to defer[40] your case. Perhaps he can provide you with a perfect[50] defence against at least half the charges.[58]

122

4. The pavement around the house is defective. However,[10] it will serve for a little time longer. I should like to[20] have it repaired, but it is a difficult job for me.[30] The paving stones are too heavy for me to lift by myself[40] without great difficulty.[45]

5. Part of the reason for our lack of funds is that we have[10] some members who have not paid their annual dues. This type[20] of problem is difficult to deal with.[28]

24 Writing circles on initially hooked strokes

UNIT 1

Principle Discovery

If we write *tray* ⟨ ⟩ and *stray* ⟨ ⟩

If we write *truck* ⟨ ⟩ and *struck* ⟨ ⟩

If we write *pray* ⟨ ⟩ and *spray* ⟨ ⟩

If we write *print* ⟨ ⟩ and *sprint* ⟨ ⟩

can you discover the shorthand signs and principles used in writing the outlines for the words listed below?

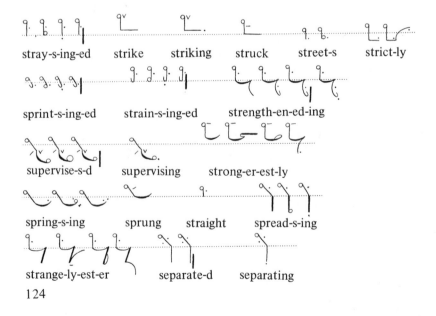

stray-s-ing-ed	strike striking	struck street-s strict-ly
sprint-s-ing-ed	strain-s-ing-ed	strength-en-ed-ing
supervise-s-d	supervising	strong-er-est-ly
spring-s-ing	sprung straight	spread-s-ing
strange-ly-est-er	separate-d	separating

124

Pitman Principles

1. To add S to the straight double consonant strokes PR, BR, TR, DR, etc., close the hook as in *stray* and *spray* . The circle now includes the R sound.

SKILL-BUILDING PLAN 1

Reading and Writing Practice

1. Read the shorthand outlines in this Unit, preferably repeating the words out loud.
2. Cover the printed words and read the shorthand outlines.
3. Write the shorthand outlines until you can write them easily and quickly without hesitation.
4. Write the shorthand outlines from dictation. Keep your text open as you write. Refer to your text whenever necessary.
5. Read the shorthand you have taken from dictation.

YOUR AIM: TO WRITE 60 WORDS A MINUTE

UNIT 2

Reading and Writing Practice

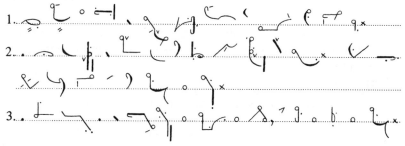

See page 126 for the key to these sentences.

Building Reading and Writing Skills

1. Read each sentence until you can read it fluently.
2. Read all the sentences as a unit. Are you reading them without hesitation?
3. Practise writing each sentence in shorthand until you can write it easily and rapidly.
4. Write all the sentences once as a unit.

Building Dictation Skills

1. Practise writing each sentence from dictation. As you write, keep your text open for easy reference.
2. Read the shorthand you have written in your notebook.

Note: When you have completed the sentences, follow the same plan when practising a paragraph or letter.

YOUR AIM: TO WRITE 80 WORDS A MINUTE

Key to Reading and Writing Practice

1. Mr. Strong has agreed to supervise the children from[10] that school as they cross the street.
2. The men have decided to strike if their demands are not[10] satisfied by spring. They are gaining support for their cause[20] and their strength is spreading.
3. The task of keeping the two groups separated is strictly[10] his responsibility, and the strain is testing[20] his strength.

Unit 3

Principle Discovery

If we write *extra*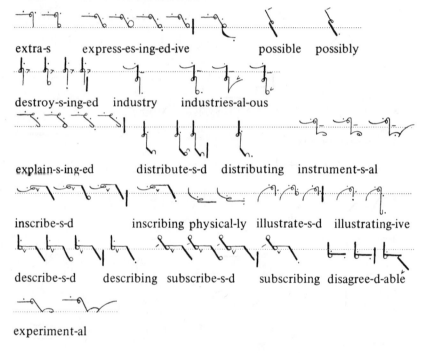

If we write *express*

If we write *possible*

If we write *explain*

can you discover the shorthand signs and principles used in writing the outlines for the words listed below?

extra-s   express-es-ing-ed-ive   possible   possibly

destroy-s-ing-ed   industry   industries-al-ous

explain-s-ing-ed   distribute-s-d   distributing   instrument-s-al

inscribe-s-d   inscribing physical-ly illustrate-s-d illustrating-ive

describe-s-d   describing subscribe-s-d   subscribing disagree-d-able

experiment-al

Pitman Principle

1.   The hook and the S-circle must be shown in the middle of a word. Note how these are shown in words like *disagree*   *subscribe* and *prescribe* .

Master Unit 3 by following Skill-Building Plan 1 on page 125.

Unit 4

Reading and Writing Practice

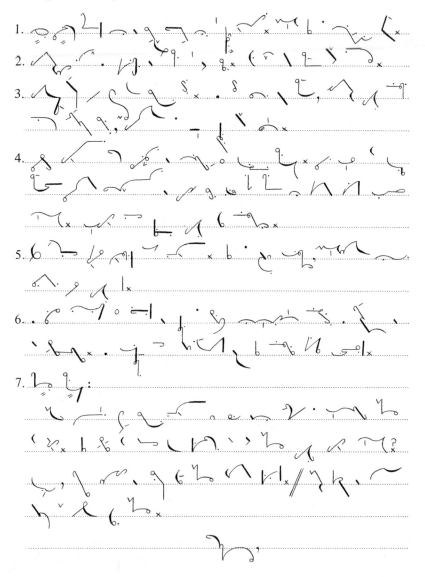

See page 129 for the key to this Unit.

Master Unit 4 by following Skill-Building Plan 2 on page 126.

Unit 5

Developing Transcription Skills

To develop your Transcribing Skill follow the Transcription Skill-Building Plan on page 103.

Key to Reading and Writing Practice

1. Mr. Silver asked me to supervise the group meeting[10] on Tuesday morning. I know that it is an important[20] job.
2. We hope that you will not allow the children to stray on[10] to the streets. They might be struck by the cars.[17]
3. We have just bought our flowers for spring planting. The plants seem[10] to be strong, and we hope that with extra care and proper[20] spraying, we will have a good display by summer.[28]
4. He has been working very seriously to improve[10] his physical strength. He knows that if he is stronger he[20] will be more likely to win the sprint events at the track[30] meet which will be held next month. No one can disagree with[40] this experiment.
5. This is the organ which was illustrated in the catalogue.[10] It is a beautiful instrument, and I know that you[20] will have many happy hours with it.[26]
6. The sales manager has agreed to distribute a special[10] memorandum explaining the problem to all subscribers.[20] The industry cannot afford to have its express charges[30] increased.
7. Dear Miss Strange:

    I have been looking through the spring catalogue[10] you sent to me and there are a number of items that[20] I want. Do you suppose that I can have delivery[30] of all the items within one month? If not, perhaps you[40] will want to separate those items that will be delayed.[50]

    I hope that it will not be too long before I receive[60] these items.

    Very truly yours,[66]

25 Doubling strokes

Unit 1

If the word *matter* is written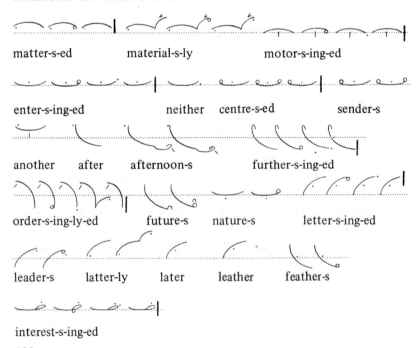

If the word *order* is written

If the word *another* is written

If the word *future* is written

can you discover the shorthand signs and principles used in writing the outlines for the words listed below?

matter-s-ed   material-s-ly   motor-s-ing-ed

enter-s-ing-ed   neither   centre-s-ed   sender-s

another   after   afternoon-s   further-s-ing-ed

order-s-ing-ly-ed   future-s   nature-s   letter-s-ing-ed

leader-s   latter-ly   later   leather   feather-s

interest-s-ing-ed

130

Pitman Principles

1. Curved strokes are doubled in length to add the sounds TR, DR, THR, thr, and TURE.

Master Unit 1 by following Skill-Building Plan 1 on page 125.

Unit 2

Reading and Writing Practice

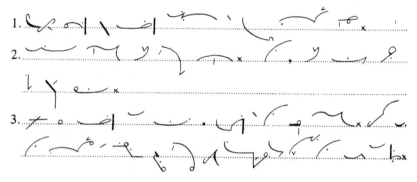

See below for the key to these sentences.

Master the sentences in Unit 2 by following Skill-Building Plan 2 on page 126.

Key to Reading and Writing Practice

1. Everyone seemed to be interested in the matter of[10] future material costs.[15]
2. In another month I shall order the motor. Later,[10] I shall enter the races at the boat centre.[18]
3. Our company is interested in entering the[10] field of leather goods manufacture. We will need leather[20] materials and expect to place orders with factories[30] for the lighter-weight leather now in demand.[48]

UNIT 3

Principle Discovery

If the word *picture* is written ....

If the word *painter* is written ....

If the word *operator* is written...........

If the word *kinder* is written ....

can you discover the shorthand signs and principles used in writing the outlines for the words listed below?

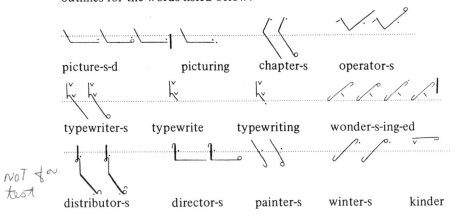

picture-s-d   picturing   chapter-s   operator-s

typewriter-s   typewrite   typewriting   wonder-s-ing-ed

distributor-s   director-s   painter-s   winter-s   kinder

NOT for test

Pitman Principles

1.   A straight stroke is doubled to add the sounds of TR, DR, THR, and TURE if it follows another stroke as in *picture* .... or has a final hook as in *painter* ....

Master Unit 3 by following Skill-Building Plan 1 on page 125.

UNIT 4

Phrases

1.   In phrases a stroke may be doubled for the addition of *there*, *their*, and *dear*, as in:

I have been   I have been there   I know   I know there is

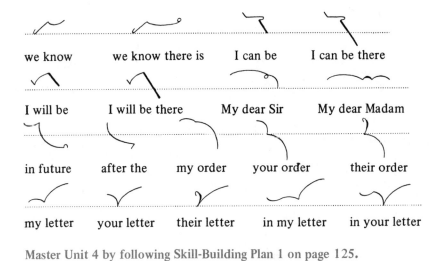

we know	we know there is	I can be	I can be there
I will be	I will be there	My dear Sir	My dear Madam
in future	after the	my order	your order	their order
my letter	your letter	their letter	in my letter	in your letter

Master Unit 4 by following Skill-Building Plan 1 on page 125.

Unit 5

Reading and Writing Practice

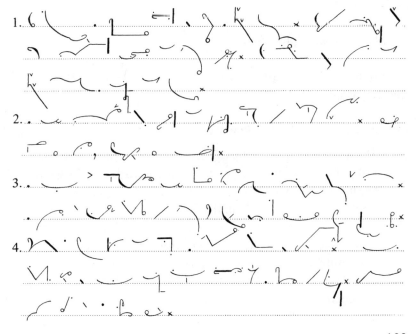

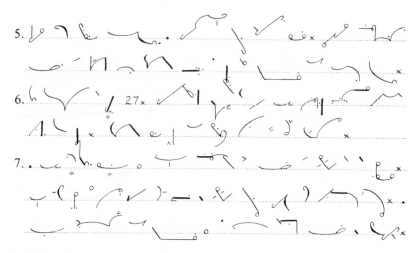

See below for the key to this Unit.

Master Unit 5 by following Skill-Building Plan 2 on page 126.

Unit 6

Developing Transcription Skills

To develop your Transcribing Skills follow the Transcription Skill-Building Plan on page 103.

Key to Reading and Writing Practice

1. This afternoon the directors agreed to purchase the[10] typewriter firm. They were impressed by the very marked[20] increase in orders recently. They expect to be the[30] leader in the typewriter manufacturing industry[40] in the future.
2. The new materials being used in children's clothing[10] are of much lighter weight. Since the cost is less, everyone is[20] interested.
3. The nature of the government's new tax laws will have an[10] important bearing on the matter. The leaders of[20] various parties are ordering their voters to meet[30] at centres throughout the different cities.[38]

4. There will be a further delay in getting the operators[10] back to work. Neither party wants to enter into[20] another agreement until the terms are changed. We know[30] there is little chance of a settlement soon.[38]

5. It was very pleasant interviewing the well-known painter[10] of winter scenes. He was extremely interesting and[20] told me that he will be giving a display of his[30] pictures in the near future.[35]

6. Thank you for your letter of June 27. We arc[10] pleased to tell you that our new illustrated catalogs[20] are now ready for distributing. They will be sent out[30] in special letter-size folders.[36]

7. The new Art Center is another example of the[10] interest and support of all citizens. No other[20] city has leaders who are so eager to support painters[30] with their regular orders. The nature of the material[40] in the pictures is a matter of great interest to[50] everyone.

26 Writing the sound of SHUN

UNIT 1

Principle Discovery

If the word *motion* is written ....⌐⌐....
If the word *collection* is written ...⌐‿‿....
If the word *section* is written ..⌐‿.
If the word *operation* is written ⌐∨⌐
If the word *addition* is written ...⌐

can you discover the shorthand signs and principles used in writing the outlines for the words listed below?

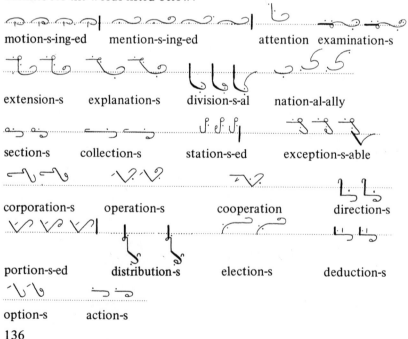

motion-s-ing-ed   mention-s-ing-ed   attention   examination-s

extension-s   explanation-s   division-s-al   nation-al-ally

section-s   collection-s   station-s-ed   exception-s-able

corporation-s   operation-s   cooperation   direction-s

portion-s-ed   distribution-s   election-s   deduction-s

option-s   action-s

136

Pitman Principles

1. A large hook expresses the sound of SHUN.
2. It is written inside curves.
3. While it may be attached to either side of a straight stroke, the preferred forms are illustrated.

Master Unit 1 by following Skill-Building Plan 1 on page 125.

Unit 2

Reading and Writing Practice

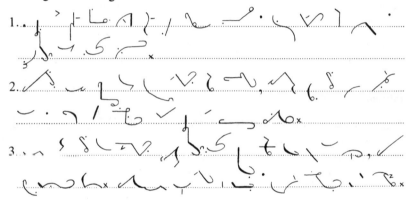

See below for the key to these sentences.

Master Unit 2 by following Skill-Building Plan 2 on page 126.

Key to Reading and Writing Practice

1. The distribution of the total tax load so that each[10] person carries a fair portion of it will be an issue[20] in the national election.[26]
2. We are planning new directions for the future operation[10] of this corporation, and we hope that these plans will[20] result in a very large extension of our[30] distribution and collection services.[38]
3. Now that the plans for cooperation with the national[10] division of this company have been put in motion,[20] we are free to mention them. We have now no option but[30] to give a full explanation to all employees.[40]

UNIT 3

Principle Discovery

If the word *position* is written ....✓....

If the word *organization* is written ....⌐____ℓ

If the word *transition* is written ....↑

can you discover the shorthand signs and principles used in writing the outlines for the words listed below?

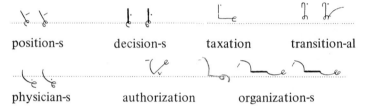

position-s	decision-s	taxation	transition-al
physician-s	authorization	organization-s	

Pitman Principles

1. When the sound of SHUN follows the S or NS circle, it is expressed by a small hook written opposite the circle.
2. When required, the S circle is written inside the hook as in *positions* ✓ .

Master Unit 3 by following Skill-Building Plan 1 on page 125.

Unit 4

Building Vocabulary Skills

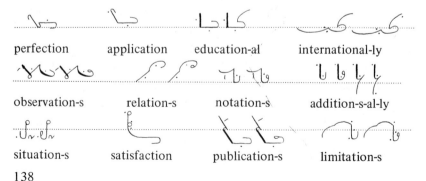

perfection	application	education-al	international-ly
observation-s	relation-s	notation-s	addition-s-al-ly
situation-s	satisfaction	publication-s	limitation-s

138

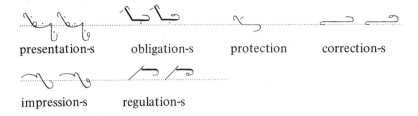

presentation-s   obligation-s   protection   correction-s

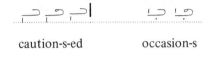

impression-s   regulation-s

Note: Put in the vowels in similar outlines.

caution-s-ed   occasion-s

Pitman Pacers

information   therefore

Master Unit 4 by following Skill-Building Plan 1 on page 125.

UNIT 5

Reading and Writing Practice

1.

2.

3.

4.

5.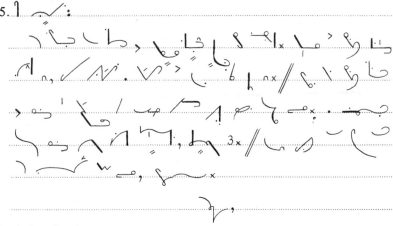

See below for the key to this Unit.

Master Unit 5 by following Skill-Building Plan 2 on page 126.

Unit 6

Developing Transcription Skills

To develop your Transcribing Skill follow the Transcription Skill-Building Plan on page 103.

Key to Reading and Writing Practice

1. The extension of the expressway through the centre of[10] the city gives rise to serious limitations on[20] the sale of homes in this section of the city.[28]
2. However, many members of the council gave very[10] sound explanations and observations in favour of[20] the present plans.
3. The additional information about the National[10] Entrance Examination will be sent to you as soon[20] as it is ready for distribution. A full explanation[30] of how the decisions are made will be given[40] in this publication. We hope these decisions will[50] improve the regulations.[55]
4. Now that we are ready for action, this material[10] will be distributed through national newspapers and[20] on national, international, and private[30] television.

5. Dear Mary:

   Your application for admission to the[10] Business Education Division has been accepted.[20] Because of the special deduction allowed you, we are[30] returning the portion of the fee which is due you.

   Please[40] pay special attention to the section on publications[50] which includes the regulation reading lists for this course.[60] The examination for your section will be held on[70] Monday, December 3.

   If you wish any further[80] information or material about the course, please let[90] me know.

                    Yours truly,

27 Writing the sounds of KW, GW, and WH

Unit 1

Principle Discovery

If the word *equip* is written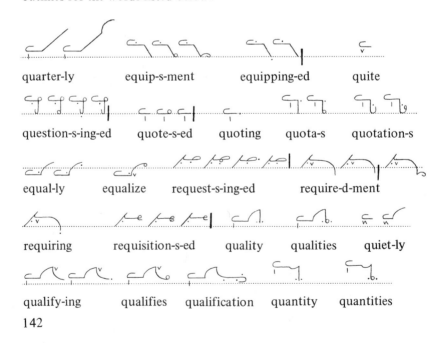

If the word *Guelph* is written

If the word *request* is written

If the word *quality* is written

can you discover the shorthand signs and principles used in writing the outlines for the words listed below?

quarter-ly   equip-s-ment   equipping-ed   quite

question-s-ing-ed   quote-s-ed   quoting   quota-s   quotation-s

equal-ly   equalize   request-s-ing-ed   require-d-ment

requiring   requisition-s-ed   quality   qualities   quiet-ly

qualify-ing   qualifies   qualification   quantity   quantities

142

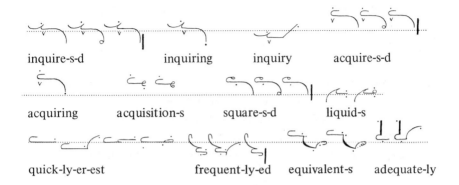

inquire-s-d   inquiring   inquiry   acquire-s-d

acquiring   acquisition-s   square-s-d   liquid-s

quick-ly-er-est   frequent-ly-ed   equivalent-s   adequate-ly

Pitman Principle

A large hook added to ⎯⎯ and ⎯⎯ expresses the sound of KW ⌐⎯ and GW ⌐⎯

Master Unit 1 by following Skill-Building Plan 1 on page 125.

Unit 2

Reading and Writing Practice

See page 144 for the key to these sentences.

Master Unit 2 by following Skill-Building Plan 2 on page 126.

Key to Reading and Writing Practice

1. I should like to question the price you have quoted for the[10] equipment ordered on our requisition dated[20] December 10. We have a quotation from Guelph Iron Works[30] for similar equipment for $200 less[40] than your price.
2. Can you meet our equipment requirements at the new price[10] quoted? If not, we shall have to purchase equipment of[20] equivalent quality from another supplier,[30] and we shall have to do it very quickly.[38]
3. We have been requisitioning our liquid fuel supplies[10] from The Square Deal Oil Company on a regular basis.[20] Can you supply sufficient liquid fuel of equivalent[30] quality which will meet our fuel requirements[40] adequately?

Unit 3

Pitman Principle

The sound of WH is represented by the sign ⟋ as in:

| when | where | while | whilst | awhile | why |

| whether | white | wheel | what |

Note: Where convenient, the stroke ⎸ is used to express the word *attention* in phrases as in:

your attention   my attention   early attention   earliest attention

Master Unit 3 by following Skill-Building Plan 1 on page 125.

UNIT 4

Reading and Writing Practice

1.

2.

3.

4.

5.

6.

7. Mr. A. Dunn
   37 Worth Road
   London, Ontario

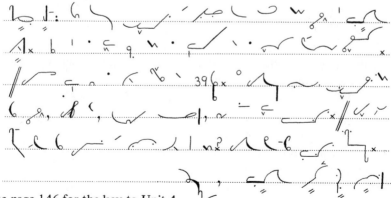

See page 146 for the key to Unit 4.

Master Unit 4 by following Skill-Building Plan 2 on page 126.

Unit 5

Developing Transcription Skills

To develop your Transcribing Skill follow the Transcription Skill-Building Plan on page 103.

1. We should like to inquire about your prices. Can you[10] send me a quotation on small quantities?[18]
2. We frequently have difficulty in knowing where we[10] can order our supplies in small quantities.[18]
3. We are interested in learning when we can expect[10] delivery after you have received our request for[20] shipment.
4. It is often necessary for us to acquire[10] this equipment quite quickly. Will you quote us a price on[20] this kind of equipment and let us know whether we can[30] expect quicker delivery. Please give this matter your[40] earliest attention.
5. We shall be happy to supply quotations on this[10] equipment and can guarantee quick delivery. May I[20] draw your attention to our new price list which is enclosed[30] with this letter.
6. The quarterly sales of your department have increased[10] greatly since the acquisition of this machine. Thank you for[20] bringing this sales report to my attention.[28]
7. Mr. A. Dunn
   37 Worth Road
   London, Ontario
   Dear Mr. Dunn:
   Thank you for your inquiry and request[10] for information about the house on Guelph Road. It is[20] on a quiet street about a quarter of a mile from[30] the high school.
   We can quote you a low price of[40] $39,000. As we have had many inquiries about[50] this house, we suggest that, if you are interested, you[60] should act quite quickly.
   Why not drop over this week and let[70] me show it to you? We have several others equally[80] attractive.

   Yours very truly,
Guelph Real Estate Limited[90]

28 Writing the sounds of CON, COM, CUM, and COG

Unit 1

Principle Discovery

If the word *control* is written _____

If the word *confirm* is written _____

If the word *community* is written _____

can you discover the shorthand signs and principles used in writing the outlines for the words listed below?

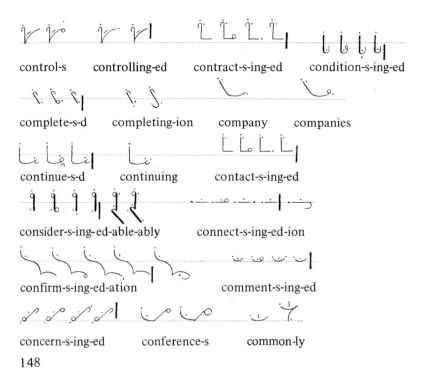

control-s   controlling-ed   contract-s-ing-ed   condition-s-ing-ed

complete-s-d   completing-ion   company   companies

continue-s-d   continuing   contact-s-ing-ed

consider-s-ing-ed-able-ably   connect-s-ing-ed-ion

confirm-s-ing-ed-ation   comment-s-ing-ed

concern-s-ing-ed   conference-s   common-ly

148

Pitman Principles

1. The sounds CON and COM at the beginning of a word are expressed by a light dot written at the beginning of the first stroke in the word.
2. The position of a word is determined by the first vowel sound following CON or COM as in *condition* ⌐ and *contract* ⌐ .

Master Unit 1 by following Skill-Building Plan 1 on page 125.

UNIT 2

Principle Discovery

If the word *discontinue* is written ....

If the word *recommend* is written ....

If the word *recognize* is written ....

If the word *circumference* is written ....

can you discover the shorthand signs and principles used in writing the outlines for the words listed below?

discontinue-s-d	discontinuing	incomplete	uncommon-ly

recommend-s-ing-ed-ation	reconsider-s-ed	disconnect-s-ing-ed

uncomfortable	recognize-s-d	recognizing	recognition

circumstance-s

PHRASES

we are confident	we shall continue	I will consider	this committee

Pitman Principles

1. In the middle of a word the sounds of CON, COM, CUM, and COG are expressed by disjoining the stroke preceding these sounds.
2. In phrases the sounds of CON and COM are indicated by writing outlines close together.

Master Unit 2 by following Skill-Building Plan 1 on page 125.

UNIT 3

Reading and Writing Practice

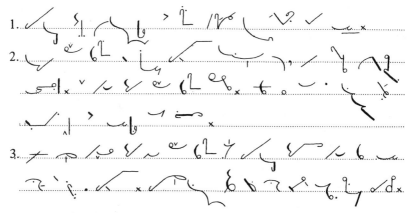

See below for the key to these sentences.

Master Unit 3 by following Skill-Building Plan 2 on page 126.

Key to Reading and Writing Practice

1. We are confident that the committee will confirm the[10] conditions of the contract which controls the future[20] operations of our new company.[27]
2. If we sign this contract to continue the work for[10] another year, our profits will be considerably[20] increased. I recommend that we sign this contract as soon[30] as possible. This company is in a favourable[40] position to carry out all the new conditions in[50] the agreement.

150

3. Our company must recognize that we should not sign this[10] contract until we are confident that we can recommend[20] this new method of completing the work. We must confirm[30] that this is the best method to use in these strange circumstances.[40]

UNIT 4

Building Vocabulary Skill

commit-s   committing-ed   committee-s   convenient-ce

conclude-s-d   concluding   compete-s-d   competing-ition

contain-s-ed   comfort-s-ing-ed-able   compensation   construct-s-ing-ed-ion

contribute-s-d   contribution   confuse-s-d   confusing-ion

Master Unit 4 by following Skill-Building Plan 1 on page 125.

UNIT 5

Reading and Writing Practice

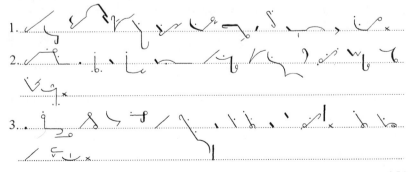

1.

2.

3.

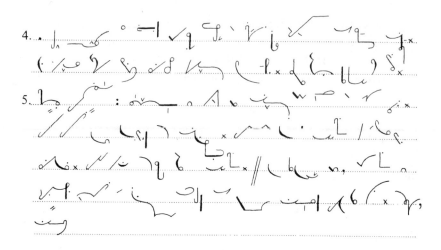

4. ...

5. ...

See below for the key to this Unit.

Master Unit 5 by following Skill-Building Plan 2 on page 126.

UNIT 6

Developing Transcription Skills

To develop your Transcribing Skill follow the Transcription Skill-Building Plan on page 103.

1. We are confident that we will be able to control[10] the competition between the various groups who plan[20] to come to the conference.[25]
2. We expect the committees to continue to make[10] recommendations which will confirm their concern about the[20] conditions in this part of the community.[28]
3. The construction companies responsible for the[10] accident are prepared to pay compensation to all[20] concerned. Compensation payments are quite common.[28]
4. The town council has agreed to reconsider the[10] question of controlling conditions of work in the[20] construction industry. They recognize that there are special[30] circumstances which require further study. It is possible[40] that they may discontinue their plans.[46]

5.   Dear Miss Wilson:

    Some time ago you wrote to us inquiring[10] about the cost of oil heating. We are wondering[20] if you have completed your investigation. We now[30] have a new contract which offers complete service. We would[40] recommend your consideration of this new contract.[50]

    If it is convenient to you, I will contact you on[60] Wednesday morning and confirm the information contained[70] in the booklet enclosed with this letter.

Yours truly,[80]

Enc.

Pitman Pacers

Lesson 1 None

Lesson 2

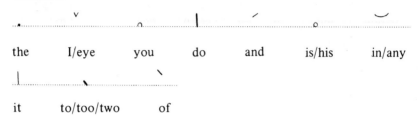

the   I/eye   you   do   and   is/his   in/any

it   to/too/two   of

Lesson 3

a/an   that   thing   anything   nothing   something

Lesson 4

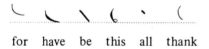

for   have   be   this   all   thank

Lesson 5

yesterday   as/has   but   put

Lesson 6

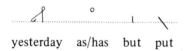

will   we

Lesson 7

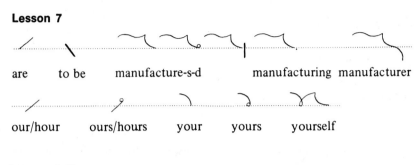

are   to be   manufacture-s-d   manufacturing   manufacturer

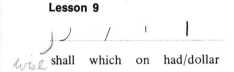

our/hour   ours/hours   your   yours   yourself

Lesson 8 None

Lesson 9

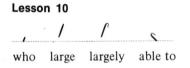

wise   shall   which   on   had/dollar

Lesson 10

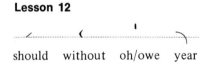

who   large   largely   able to

Lesson 11 None

Lesson 12

should   without   oh/owe   year

Lesson 13

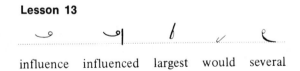

influence   influenced   largest   would   several

Lesson 14

dear   larger   accord   almost   always   also
               according
               according to

Lesson 15

think

Lesson 16 None

Lesson 17 None

Lesson 18

how

Lesson 19 None

Lesson 20

cannot

Lesson 21

owing   together   altogether   responsible-ility   satisfactory   Balance

Lesson 22

very   there/their   more   before

156

Lesson 23 None

Lesson 24 None

Lesson 25 None

Lesson 26

information   therefore

People

Appendix

In the classic edition of Pitman shorthand there are several ways of indicating a past tense. In SHORTERHAND, as presented in this text, all past tenses are represented by a single principle— the disjoined stroke. Since SHORTERHAND is a development of the original Pitman shorthand system, it incorporates within its theory many of the original principles of classic Pitman.

For instance, it is theoretically possible within this SHORTERHAND system to indicate past tenses in the classic Pitman manner.

In classic Pitman shorthand past tenses may be formed by
(a)   using the ST loop as in *pace, paced* and *lease, leased*
(b)   halving simple strokes as in *laugh, laughed* and *copy, copied*

In order to preserve the closest possible relationship between the original outline and its derivatives, the presentation in this text follows consistently the principle of the disjoined stroke for all past tenses. This approach was followed in the belief that the disjoining principle introduces a consistent pattern which reduces the learning load and eliminates the necessity of choosing between alternative methods of representing past tenses. Nevertheless it is possible to represent past tenses in SHORTERHAND using principles (a) and (b) outlined above.

In determining the position of the SHUN hook on straight strokes the following principles have been applied:
(a)   On the side opposite an initial circle or hook;
(b)   On the side opposite to the last vowel if there is no initial circle or hook;
(c)   On the right side of T, D, or J.

9 10 11 12   001310   83 82 81 80 79